Praise for Breakfast Wine

"Vivid in her details, unblinking in her honesty, Alex Poppe has rendered a complex, interwoven personal narrative that is urgent and moving at every turn. Its images precise, its language fierce yet lyrical, its heart on its sleeve, *Breakfast Wine* sets its stakes on a whole range of human experience. In a line that we want —that we need—to be true, Poppe insists, 'In the bubble of breath and body we form, there is exhilaration and release.' If that is so, then *Breakfast Wine* plunges toward the marrow of that very way of being."

—**Richard Deming**
author of *This Exquisite Loneliness*

"*Breakfast Wine* is an extraordinarily immersive memoir from a writer with a first-class mind. I was struck again and again by Alex Poppe's insights and her experiences related to the complexities of living abroad as a single woman, in particular, the gender-based hypocrisies and sexual predation (and its apologists) she encountered. This is also a book about finding one's way in the world as an artist and an intellectual. *Breakfast Wine* is a terrific book deserving of a huge readership."

—**Christine Sneed**
author of *Please Be Advised*

"In a time when America's role in the world seems as nebulous as ever, *Breakfast Wine* confronts that issue with blazing consideration and rare grace. Due to her work as an English-language instructor and humanitarian-aid volunteer in Kurdistan and beyond, Alex Poppe put herself out in the world in ways so few Americans are ever willing to. Yet it's her voice, literary and direct and yearning, that'll linger with you long after you finish her story."

— **Matt Gallagher**
author of *Daybreak*

"A remarkable braiding of the geopolitical and intimately personal, Alex Poppe's memoir, *Breakfast Wine*, plumbs the depths of yearning. Adventure, knowledge, purpose, understanding, agency, belonging—these are just a few of the things Poppe yearns toward as she travels the world and (un)settles in

Iraq as a teacher during the complicated tumult of the past couple of decades. Told in innovative structures and exquisite language, *Breakfast Wine* is a page turner; it is an eye opener."

— **Patricia Ann McNair**
author of *The Temple of Air*

"While teaching Kurdish teens and young adults in northern Iraq, Alex Poppe's passion for writing helped her address a tough and harsh reality. In fast-paced, lively, and often blunt language, Poppe shines a light on people whose lives are forever altered by wars they never chose. Readers will find, in *Breakfast Wine*, an unusual contribution to antiwar literature and a lively call to uphold human rights."

— **Kathy Kelly**
three-time Nobel Peace Prize nominee

"*Breakfast Wine* is a fascinating and moving account of an American woman living in northern Iraq during a deeply formative time in her life. The writing is beautiful, devastating, tender and often funny. Through Poppe's eyes there is little judgement, only observation of humanity in a violent society, where people struggle deeply but are resilient, full of the capacity for joy, wonder, and forgiveness."

—**Lisa Cupolo**
author of *Have Mercy on Us*

"Alex Poppe's *Breakfast Wine* follows a series of accolades and prize-winning books. This one should win her a prize for bravery. *Breakfast Wine* is an engaging, intimate, eye-opening portrait of not only the dangers of traveling abroad but more so of a singularly lively and courageous young woman who refuses to surrender her desire to experience and know the world despite its frequent ugliness and evil."

—**Randall Silvis**
author of *Two Days Gone*

"*Breakfast Wine* is immersive, honest, and completely absorbing. Expertly composed, its stories cover an astonishing range from displacement to home, from heart-wrenching tragedies to unexpected levities. At every step of this gripping journey, Poppe considers complex lives and places with empathic attention to detail, emotion, and meaning. This is an extraordinary work that will reverberate long after reading."

—Charlie Hailey
author of *Campsite: Architectures of Duration and Place*

"In *Breakfast Wine*, Alex Poppe takes readers on a decade-long odyssey, teaching students in war-torn Iraq. Through her eyes, we experience the trials and triumphs of a female Westerner striving to assimilate into a society that is often unwelcoming. Whether fleeing from earthquakes or grappling with personal tragedy, Poppe's journey of self-discovery is a feast for the senses. This captivating memoir is both heartbreaking and heartwarming—an intoxicating read that invites you to drink in every moment."

—Randy Richardson
author of *Havana Hangover*

"With self-effacing humor and unflinching candor, Alex Poppe weaves a tangled and tortuous web of remembrances from her decade spent teaching in northern Iraq. *Breakfast Wine* deftly interweaves journalistic arm's length reporting on cultural differences and political events with deeply emotional first-person perspectives on the impacts those differences and events had on her and others. The effect is both heartening and heartbreaking as her taut tales whip you from one life-altering moment to the next. Reliving this decade with Poppe will have you questioning whether you have ever really lived at all."

—David R. Roth
author of *The Femme Fatale Hypothesis*

"*Breakfast Wine* is a journey by an open-eyed traveler who peels away layers of the complex worlds she enters. The book interweaves perceptive insights with personal reflections; propelled by love and "warrior anger," as she aptly terms it. Adventurous, curious, vulnerable, Poppe opens a window on Iraqi Kurdistan in this up-close and personal account of the challenges of navigating other cultures as a single white female. She draws precise and incisive portraits of wild characters and ordinary Iraqis, we relish her ferocious energy, her clarity, and her commitment to living intensely as she "tries on" different selves This heartful account is told with insight and acuity, spiced with vivid, inventive language, and is by turns laugh-out-loud hilarious and deeply tender. We know her from the first sentence, but we learn more and more about her fascinating journey. The book reflects Poppe's thirst for honesty, social justice, and living an authentic life while staying true to her nomad nature. *Breakfast Wine* is a wild ride through Kurdish Iraq, by turns tragic, adventurous, hilarious and tender, written by a true explorer."

—**Ellen Kaplan**
editor and co-contributor of
Theatre Responds to Social Trauma: Chasing the Demon

"In immediate break-speed prose, *Breakfast Wine* immerses us in a fugue-like world of confusion and contradictions. Through her vivid and unflinching narrative, Poppe captures the resilience of the human spirit and the search for identity amidst chaos. *Breakfast Wine* is a testament to the power of courage, reflection, and the unyielding quest for meaning in an unpredictable world, revealing what it means to be fully alive and engaged in our choices and the world around us."

—**Judith Turner Yamamoto**
author of *Loving the Dead and Gone*

"This beautifully written memoir, told in vignettes of the author's experience in northern Iraq, is filled with poignant and raw moments that depict the stark reality of the life the author left behind. The reader is taken along with Poppe as she provides humanitarian aid to refugees in a nearby village and when she leads a discussion of *The Handmaid's Tale* with her students (including one woman wearing a hijab). The author went to Iraq because something was missing in her own life. I'm sure the many lives she touched while there are grateful that she did."

—**Michelle Paris**
author of *Eat Dessert First*

Also by Alex Poppe

Duende
Jinwar and Other Stories
Moxie
Girl, World

Breakfast Wine

Breakfast Wine

*A Memoir of Chasing an Unconventional Life
and Finding a Way Home*

Alex Poppe

Apprentice House Press
Loyola University Maryland

Copyright © 2025 by Alex Poppe

All rights reserved. No part of this book may be reproduced or transmitted in any form or by any means, electronic or mechanical, including photocopy, recording, or any information storage and retrieval system, without prior permission from the publisher (except by reviewers who may quote brief passages).

First Edition

Casebound ISBN: 978-1-62720-593-1
Paperback ISBN: 978-1-62720-594-8
Ebook ISBN: 978-1-62720-595-5

Cover Design by Louis Mandrapilias
Internal Design by J.P. Stromberg
Editorial Development by Molly Gerard
Promotional Development by Olivia DiTroia

Published by Apprentice House Press

Apprentice House Press
Loyola University Maryland

Loyola University Maryland
4501 N. Charles Street, Baltimore, MD 21210
410.617.5265
www.ApprenticeHouse.com
info@ApprenticeHouse.com

Disclaimer

Memory is constructed, opened, closed, forgotten, reopened, and well-interrogated. This is a work of memory, which fades and warps with retelling, and experience, which is subjective. Dialogue is approximate and appears in quotation marks for the ease of the reader. To facilitate story, some events, sequences, and characters have been condensed.

Names have been changed or omitted to protect me.

"Arabic for Dummies" originally appeared in the anthology, *The White Picket Fence: Stories of Individuality as Rebelliousness,* published by FlowerSong Press; "Five Weeks" was originally published in the *Amsterdam Review*; "Board Porn" and "All Together Now, Penis!" were originally published as "'All Together Now, Penis!': Teaching Feminist Literature in Patriarchal Iraq" in *Bust*; "Don't Say a Word", "Down the Rabbit Hole", and "The Impossible Do-Over" were published as "Reprieve" in the *Los Angeles Review*; "Tethered" was originally published by the *Laurel Review*; and "Ode to WhatsApp" was published by Medium's *The Startup*.

For My Dad,
Fred Wolfgang Poppe
1933-2020

"We look at the world once, in childhood. The rest is memory."
—Louise Gluck, "Nostos"

"We travel, some of us forever, to seek other places, other lives, other souls."
— Anaïs Nin

Contents

Foreword
Liminal Spaces xix

One
New York City 2011
Erbil, Kurdistan, Iraq 2011
Arabic for Dummies 3
While Utu is Halfway to Hawaii 12

Two
Erbil, Kurdistan, Iraq 2011
A Pleasant Addition to Any Classroom 21
Since You Arrived, My Heart Stopped Belonging to Me 25

Three
Erbil, Kurdistan, Iraq 2012
Five Weeks 41

Four
Erbil, Kurdistan, Iraq 2012-2013
Leipzig, Germany 2013-2015
Pied Pipers 61
A Chance Object Fabricates a Life 65
Camping 69
Decamping 76

Five
Sulaimaniyah, Kurdistan, Iraq 2015

Board Porn   85
All Together Now, "Penis!"   97

Six
Sulaimaniayh, Kurdistan, Iraq 2017

"Men Grow Old and Have Bored or Stupid Sons." -Herbert Butler   107
Stardust and Voodoo   113
The Go Bag   120

Seven
Baghdad, Iraq 2018

Wasta   129
The Second Wife   136
You Call Yourself a Feminist   143

Eight
Sulaimaniayh, Kurdistan, Iraq 2019

Don't Say a Word   151
Down the Rabbit Hole   155
The Impossible Do-Over   162

Nine
Naples, Italy 2019

Tethered   171

Ten
Sulaimaniayh, Kurdistan, Iraq 2020-2021

Ode to WhatsApp   187
Breakfast Wine   196
Departure   203

Cheat Sheet   211
Acknowledgements   215
About the Author   217

Foreword
Liminal Spaces

When I was a high school teacher of world history, I designed a role-playing lesson for my students about the postwar occupation of Iraq, a subject of fascination to me. Students played US aid workers, occupation soldiers, and Iraqi civilians of various ethnicities trying to build a fragile peace in a war-torn region in the country's north. Inevitably, the complexities of this war-torn space would bring their efforts to grief, hopefully to teach my American students about the immense difficulties of this undertaking.

Years later, and after I left teaching, I met Alex Poppe, an eclectic world traveler recently come to Tulsa, Oklahoma to work remotely. She could have easily been a character out of my lesson. *Breakfast Wine* chronicles her experiences traversing the distance between her upbringing in an American immigrant household and the conflict zones of northern Iraq, where she worked as a teacher. It's a story of boundary-crossings: between the West and the rich mosaic of the Middle East, between patriarchy and feminism, between generations. The result is a remarkably relevant portrait of the dilemma of modern existence: how to map out and maintain stable borders in a world of shifting lines and uncertainty.

As a Western woman teaching privileged kids English in Iraqi Kurdistan, she had to navigate the ancient codes of tribal values, family connections (or "wasta"), and gender expectations to promote a humanistic and student-centered approach to education and achievement with her students. As an aid worker in conflict zones, she experienced the impact of US foreign policy and ancient fault lines on the lives of ordinary people trying to survive. And as an unconventional and unmarried woman, she navigates the challenges of relationships in multiple cultures without any clear map or guidebook.

Consider this passage:

"Raised by an immigrant father and a traditional homemaker in the 1970s, I wasn't taught how to show up for myself and ask for what I wanted. My learning curve was a pendulum swinging between timid hints and privilege-fueled demands until I got "the ask" right. My trip to Baghdad was the result of getting the ask right. Thanks to Rif's wasta, I was going to run a workshop on student-centered teaching at the conference which was being held at one of the oldest institutions of higher learning in the world. I was thrilled to be on my way to Baghdad, a palimpsest of dynasties, caliphs, and occupiers, treading in that liminal space between dulled grandeur and war."

In other respects, Ms. Poppe recalls the spirit of Gertrude Bell, the 20th-century chain-smoking Victorian polyglot woman who graduated from Oxford, climbed the Swiss Alps, and traversed the Middle East before and after the First World War. She was famous for her desert journeys, bringing her silver tea set on the backs of camels in case she met some sheikhs along the way. But where Gertrude Bell played a role in drawing the colonial boundaries of modern Iraq after the infamous Sykes-Picot Agreement, Poppe is an eyewitness to its erosion, and the slow creation of something new from the chaos. As a fifty-something American woman still exploring her own identity, fond of wearing designer dresses as an assertion of self, she is the ideal guide to a perplexing world. Her struggles mirror our own, and her inquiry into cultural standards challenges us to ask similar questions.

All of this is expressed through a beautifully descriptive command of language and image. Whatever the contradictions of her German-American upbringing, she received an excellent education and used it to explore the world, if not to secure herself a cozy and comfortable American existence. Maybe that's what makes her such an excellent teacher, the kind who frees you from imposed limitations and mind-forged manacles. Read her book and you'll see what I mean. Boundaries, after all, were meant to be explored.

—**John Waldron**
Member of the Oklahoma House of Representatives

One

New York City 2011
Erbil, Kurdistan, Iraq 2011

Arabic for Dummies

Hanging onto the Land Cruiser's roof rack with my left hand, I let go with my right, twisting to take photos of the stampede of children chasing us. Riding the back bumper evoked the exhilarated invincibility of youth. *This is why I came here,* I thought. *This is wh*—the truck hit a deep rut in the dirt road, and I went flying.

It was 2012. The year prior, I had moved to Kurdistan, Iraq, motivated by desperation and curiosity in equal measure. I was forty-five years old.

*

Summer 2011

I woke to the wail of New York City sirens assailing the streets. Outside my bedroom window, clouds drifted zoologically over squat, repurposed factory buildings in the early morning light. Rolling over on my air mattress, I was greeted by a steady, hissing whisper. The mattress had deflated almost to the laminate hardwood floor. The toilet flushed, the bathroom door clacked open, and the ZZ Top-bearded man from whom I sublet the bedroom padded down the hallway, probably scratching his belly.

At that time, I was the director of marketing and operations for an internet startup which provided concierge-like services for apartment buildings lacking a doorman. It was a position formidable in title only. The founder and sole other employee would interrupt strategy sessions to ponder Kim Kardashian's breast size while wolf-whistling at pictures of her tits online. My position was so poorly paid that I had to wait tables two nights a week at an unglamorous Upper West Side Italian restaurant. My fellow servers and busboys gossiped that I was an undercover agent for US Immigration and Customs Enforcement (ICE) because they didn't understand why someone like me—white, legal, and educated—was working at this under the radar restaurant at my perimenopausal age. Meanwhile, the owner's wife watched me like a hawk.

"Why haven't you bought your own place yet?' my Israeli almost-boyfriend admonished, skirting the fact that he had dealt a lot of drugs to scrape together the seed money to start his handyman business. To be fair, the equivalent of an apartment down payment was probably hanging in my closet. I suffered from a different type of Cinderella Syndrome; the belief that wearing the right dress would change my life. Many of the vintage and designer frocks I owned still bore their tags. Neither they nor I got out much.

"So, you never married or had any children?" messaged a former colleague from my business analyst days at Mobil Oil. Her daughter had just shown her how to use Facebook. My ex-colleague now lived outside of Princeton, where she'd earned her master's degree. Her daughter had decided to become an actor, which made my colleague think of me because the last time I had seen her, I was doing implausible murder mystery dinner theater in Philadelphia's Old City. How could I explain the permanent restlessness of my soul? That I hadn't married because I couldn't guarantee that my life path would run parallel to a partner's. That I thought having children was thankless. From conception, there is a tiny person kicking you as it grows, and you can't kick back.

A few days later a "How did your life turn out?" message came from a college friend I hadn't seen since 1989, when I had a terrifying perm. This friend had been named a "Women to Watch" by *Advertising Age* in the early aughts. Now, she was the regional creative director for Coca-Cola, Asia Pacific, had a daughter, and lived in a spacious high-rise in Hong Kong, where she was part of a competitive crew team. After trawling her Facebook feed, I lay on my leaking air mattress and stared at the ceiling, feeling my age settle around me. Two floors below, there had been a recent drug bust, and the super or the police or the tenant, depending on who told you the story, had removed the front door so the police wouldn't break it down the next time someone got caught dealing. A tear slid from my eye to my ear.

I had been the top grad of my university's undergraduate business school. Where had I derailed?

I tiptoed back along a mental trail of breadcrumbs to my Mobil Oil days in the early 1990s, to sharking corporate happy hours, running on a corporate track team, bumping my head on the corporate glass ceiling. Everything I heard, I had heard before, and I couldn't listen any longer. I chucked my corporate existence, along with my family's expectations, to embrace an actor's life despite never having been on a stage. Twenty-three and green, I auditioned for my first play.

From the humility of hindsight, I doubt I wanted to be an actor as much as I wanted to live a variegated, visceral artist's existence, where all the colors ran. In reality, I was more the unfulfilled housewife played by Rosanna Arquette in *Desperately Seeking Susan* than the bohemian sprite played by Madonna. Acting was a reprieve from my sheltered Catholic upbringing, an exploration of possibility where I could let desire and instinct creep. Every set was an opportunity to create family, and every performance was a playdate with an audience.

In 2003, I became friends with the writer/director Larysa

Kondracki while acting in a short film of hers. She asked me to read her new screenplay which would become her debut feature, *The Whistleblower*, starring Rachel Weisz and Vanessa Redgrave. The main character is real life Kathryn Bolkovac, a UN peacekeeper in post-war Bosnia. She outed UN officials for their role in facilitating and then covering up sex trafficking. Reading Larysa's script reignited my childhood dream to become a spy. I devoured her source material and continued down a literary rabbit hole, reading books by *New York Times* journalists and international aid workers.

Emergency Sex and Other Desperate Measures: A True Story from Hell on Earth by Kenneth Cain, Heidi Postlewait, and Andrew Thomson changed the direction of my life. In the book, Andrew, Ken, and Heidi detail their work for the UN on the frontlines of Cambodia, Somalia, Haiti, Rwanda, Bosnia, and Liberia. The authors' deployments were everything I craved: escape from the doldrums of ordinary living into adrenaline-fueled moments of feeling intensely alive. They did important work, partied like they meant it, and formed brothers-in-arms type friendships. In contrast, pursuing the chance to play someone else's life seemed frivolous and indulgent, especially when I realized I wasn't living my own. I was auditioning, occasionally performing, shopping for magic-making dresses, and waiting tables at an upscale tapas bar. I wasn't challenging my personal limitations by having new experiences.

Those vintage and designer dresses cajoled from the closet as I alternated evening play rehearsals/performances with evening wait shifts. I'd close the tapas bar at two in the morning, cab to my illegal sublet in gentrifying Williamsburg, and wake up at six to ride the subway back into Times Square to queue at Actors' Equity for a coveted audition slot. I'd race back to Williamsburg, sleep for an hour, workout, do a vocal warm-up, practice my monologue, race back to Actors' Equity, take my two minutes in the audition spotlight, and then scurry across Midtown to the tapas bar to wait another ten-hour shift. Rinse. Repeat. My actor's life had become as routine as my corporate one.

In 2005, through an aspiring playwright whose fiancée was best friends with the fiancée of the press secretary to then Secretary-General of the United Nations, Kofi Annan, I met Andrew Thomson, one of the *Emergency Sex* authors. One minute, the press secretary was offering me the chance to meet Andrew, and the next, Andrew and I were sitting in fellow *Emergency Sex* author Kenneth Cain's apartment, drinking beer as Andrew told me stories from the book, first-hand. When Andrew excused himself, I got up to peruse the titles on Ken's bookshelf, where several personal photos reproduced in *Emergency Sex* were displayed. Standing in front of the real-life objects photographed in my favorite book was an Alice *Through the Looking Glass* moment which made the fantastical looking glass world of humanitarian aid real. Metaphorically, I had climbed onto the fireplace mantle at Looking-Glass House and was poking the mirror behind it. That night propelled me to step through the mirror and enter an alternate world of expat, first as a teacher and later as an occasional humanitarian aid volunteer. I quit acting (no loss to the profession), got certified to Teach English as a Second Language (TESL) because I thought teaching abroad could be a stepping stone to aid work, and didn't look back.

My first teaching assignments in the mid-aughts—in a tiny coal mining town in southwest Poland, in a cosmopolitan Turkish port city on the Aegean, and in Ukraine's capital as the country's currency plummeted—submerged me in tidal waves of culture shock. As I rode the learning curve of my first postings, logic often seemed reversed. On ice-covered, unsalted, and unshoveled sidewalks, young Polish women wore strappy high heels, which kept their ankles in a state of constant turmoil. In the Turkish language school where I taught, the director of studies reprimanded me for cleaning my own desk. I was *severely* reprimanded when I helped an older cleaning woman carry heavy grocery bags from the elevator we had just shared to the school's canteen. A 2008 tourist guidebook to Ukraine touted its women as its greatest commodity as the International Organization for Migration (IOM) started a country-wide, anti-trafficking initiative to help trafficking victims start small businesses. I felt sorry for the uncleverly proportioned eight and nine-year-old girls I saw in Kyiv's city center, posing for pictures by a statue of Vladimir Lenin, instinctively knowing how to stand with their nascent breasts thrust forward and their lower backs arched out.

Before I went abroad, I hadn't thought much about the US's role in the world. I wanted to live outside of my culture for the same reasons I wanted an artist's life. Since I owned very little but books and designer clothing, I could easily pack up, ship out, and start over. Living abroad is more forgiving for those of us who have not found ourselves according to traditional American measures of success: spouse, children, and home ownership.

I took for granted my belief in American exceptionalism much the same way I took for granted my belief in God. I was baptized Catholic, grew up in a Catholic household, went to a Catholic grade school, and graduated from a Jesuit university. Believing in God was as reflexive as breathing. Similarly, I was indoctrinated into American exceptionalism by American ideals-led school curricula and my father's lived experience.

Dad was a true "by your bootstraps" immigrant poverty to American middle class success story. Born in Berlin in 1933, he rarely spoke about his war-scarred childhood or how he and his mother survived in bombed out Berlin during the war and its immediate aftermath. One story rescued from the ashes of forgetting has my five-year-old father running through a field in the countryside outside Berlin as Allied forces strafed it. I had a few stories about his journey to the US at age 14 and his first years in Chicago, from which I could extrapolate a life. He and my grandmother crossed the Atlantic aboard the *USAT General Henry Taylor*, a military transport ship, with support from the International Refugee Organization. Among their personal belongings, they had three US twenty-dollar bills, bought on the black market as Germany's monetary system had collapsed after the war. Hoping they weren't counterfeit, my dad rolled them into the film compartment of a Leica camera while my grandmother packed a set of eight gold-rimmed dining plates. When they reached Chicago, they sold the camera and the plates to have money to live on. Learning English at night school, passing his GED, and earning a bachelor's degree from Northwestern University, my father embodied the self-reliance and personal determination underpinning American exceptionalism, which heavily influenced my upbringing. Having attained the American Dream, he fervently believed the United States was the best country in the world.

My first expat years coincided with the first WikiLeaks publications. *Standard Operating Procedures for Camp Delta* details US practices at Guantanamo Bay detention camp. I quietly doubted a Ukrainian student who told me about a US airstrike video in which two *Reuters* reporters were killed and two children were wounded in Baghdad until I went online and read about it for myself. The children had been travelling in a van which stopped to help the airstrike victims, and the US military fired on it. One pilot is heard saying, "Well, it's their fault for bringing their kids into battle." Reading the leaks was a *Wizard of Oz*, man behind the curtain moment. The government of the country that my immigrant father credited for saving his life had violated prisoners' human rights and tried to cover up the killing of journalists and children. I was seeing the funhouse mirror image of the US that others had already recognized. The realization was a cartoon steamrolling. Deflated, I read. Suzy Hansen's *Notebooks on a Foreign Country: An American Abroad in a Post-American World* is essential reading for believers in or those disabused of American exceptionalism.

At a book signing in New York City in 2011, I met journalist Jere Van Dyk, who had been kidnapped by the Taliban and held for 45 days. Once again, the power of stories awakened my hunger for adventure, setting me on a new path. Jere talked about his time in Afghanistan, first in his youth in the 1960s, when Afghan women wore knee socks and mini-skirts in Kabul, and later in the 1980s, when Jere embedded with Jalaluddin Haqqani's *mujahideen* fighters as a freelance journalist for *The New York Times*. He returned again in the mid-aughts, at which time he was taken. He was in his 60s.

"After I got out, the FBI told me that when I went home, there'd be messages from the Taliban on my answering machine. They wanted to know if I recognized the voices," Jere told me over dinner, recounting his first moments back on US soil in a little room off of passport control at the JFK airport.

Hummus clung to a pita chip suspended halfway between my plate and my open mouth. Jere and I were sharing a meze platter at a Balkan wine delicatessen in Hell's Kitchen, where I hung onto his every word. He paused, airing out anxiety before his story resumed, spreading and loitering. Afghanistan infused him with an ecstasy of adrenaline, which was narcotic.

Thinking over his stories, I realized where I'd derailed. By the time I met Jere, I had already lived in Poland, Turkey, and Ukraine. Now, I was working as the director of marketing and operations for the man with the mammary fixation, trying to erect a superstructure of normal life. Haunted by the sense I was missing out on something, I decided to go abroad again and try on alternative selves. Reading a job advertisement for an elite international school in Kurdistan, Iraq conjured the petal-soft notes of the oud, the pungent smell of sun-roasted desert sand, and the lambent glow of bustling streets teeming with errands of mystery. Naïve and fueled by the myth of intuition, I balanced on the edge of my courage and applied.

In a pre-ISIS world, my accepting a teaching position in Kurdistan, Iraq was to swing on a rope of convention and let go. Most people, including me, hadn't heard of the Kurds or Kurdistan. When I told my restaurant patrons I was moving to Kurdistan, they thought Kurdistan was "one of those stans over there, near Russia." When I said it was in northern Iraq, they would go all silent for a moment, look at their shoes sticking to the wine-soaked floor, assume I was military, and thank me for my service. My fellow servers thought I was "just plain crazy" when they saw the *Arabic for Dummies*, which I dutifully lugged on the subway for some light reading. A punk rocker who helped me break into my apartment when my key didn't work asked me if I was CIA before he promised not to come back later and steal our computers.

Telling people about my impending move to Kurdistan was a dose of reality interrupting long blitzes of mental static. Beyond updating my vaccines and deciding which dresses to pack, I was flying blind. After all, Kurds speak Kurdish, not Arabic.

While Utu is Halfway to Hawaii

His hand cracked across my cheek. Stunned, I looked into the face of a government advisor on religious affairs to the Kurdistan Regional Government (KRG). His mouth laughed, but his eyes were flat, mean. Silence gasped like an echo from the bottom of a well as the elevator descended from a rooftop nightclub to the ground floor, where his white Range Rover was parked, a Kalashnikov tucked discreetly behind the front passenger seat. Satisfied by my docility, the advisor, whom I had met weeks before in his Chinese restaurant with a rumored brothel above, turned away from me to watch the lights flash in descending order. I did what the moment demanded. I, too, turned—to drop my hand out of sight before driving it through to his face as the doors opened, and I strode calmly into the night.

This was Kurdistan in late autumn, 2011: untamed, existing in a liminal space teeming with contradictions and open to possibility.

*

August 2011

The flight from New York to Istanbul was long, made more so by the flaming-cheeked Korean-American who plunked down in the empty seat next to me in a slow burn attempt to pick me up. I had no patience for amateurs. As he talked at me, sharing the kind of secrets that belong in a country song, I realized we'd been employed by the same school, and I wanted him to go away. Risking future bitch-branding, I strongly suggested he return to his seat. Little did I know this alcohol-infused Korean from California and I were destined to be friends.

As we deplaned in the Ataturk airport ahead of a mind-numbing layover before the flight to Kurdistan, he sidled up, fingerprinting my waist. "Let's see about finding you a shower," he said in reference to my hope that the airport lounge had shower facilities.

I decisively removed his hand from my body and sped up the stairs linking arrivals to international transfers. Small groups of pasty British men, their naked, angry scalps red and oozing, jostled through the melee of travelers. The British men were returning home after having hair transplant procedures in Turkey. Years later, a friend would haul up those same stairs on her return to Kurdistan moments before ISIS attacked the airport.

The flight from Istanbul to Erbil gave me my first taste of Kurdish aviation. Outside the small plane's window, winter-white light spangled the creaturely dark, throwing mountain ridges into relief. The Turkish Armed Forces were bombing guerilla fighters from the Kurdistan Workers' Party (PKK), who live in the mountains bearding northwest along Iran to the Turkish and Iraqi borders. Across the airplane aisle, a twenty-something Pakistani-American turned to look for someone, turned to look for someone, turned to look for someone to confirm what he suspected. He stabbed me with a stare. "Was that a bomb?"

Resolved blanketed fear and shrugged my shoulders. Right then, I understood why ignorance was bliss.

A few years later, I would fly back over Kurdistan on my way to Istanbul. In the small hours of the night, the flight attendants closed all the blinds while the pilot dimmed the interior lights and warned us not to look out the windows or lift the shades. A tense hush befell us as the flight attendants stalked the aisle, proud and quiet, like buffalo. Peeling up a side edge of the blind, I peeked out. The plane's wing was shrouded in a cloak of shale-grey darkness. The exterior lights, including the red and green ones attached to each wing, and the anti-collision beacon lights on the top and bottom of the fuselage, had been dimmed to make the plane invisible as it passed over a live conflict zone. On the ground below, the Iraqi army, with the help of the Shia-majority Popular Mobilization Forces (PMF) and US-led air strikes, fought to drive ISIS from Mosul.

Flying above active conflict instead of rerouting to a safe path is a metaphor for how Kurdish people live. They go about their daily lives no matter the circumstances. Government employees worked despite not being paid their full salaries for months at a time. The police went on strike, and nobody broke store front windows in a frenzy of looting. Schools opened while ISIS closed in on Kurdish cities. Smugglers transported counterfeit alcohol despite forced border closures in the aftermath of a failed Kurdish referendum. Shops, restaurants, bars, clubs, gyms, and swimming pools welcomed guests during the second wave of COVID-19 despite the Delta variant spawning and vaccines being in short supply.

Having lived in Kurdistan on and off for ten years, I wonder if topography is what makes the Kurds intrepid. Local folklore whispers the Zagros Mountains house the entrance to the Mesopotamian underworld. Its inhabitants live in a shadowy version of this one, eating and drinking only dry dust. At night, the Sumerian sun god Utu travels eastward under the Zagros to prepare for sunrise. By day, pirate routes crisscross the Zagros. Kurdish taxi drivers stuff cartons of cigarettes into the backpacks of Western adventure seekers, including mine, betting on Western privilege to dissuade a Turkish border crossing search. Tanker trucks smuggle Kurdish oil into Iran, defying US sanctions and bypassing profit-sharing agreements made with the central government in Baghdad. Meanwhile, hashish enters Kurdistan from the east as Utu is halfway to Hawaii.

Kurdistan's mountains have always provided sanctuary. Kurds outran Chemical Ali's poisoned apple gas and hid in the Zagros' rocky pockets during Sadaam's genocidal Anfal campaign. Evading the Turkish military, PKK fighters nestled in the avocado green crannies of Mount Qandil near Iran, where they handed out plastic bags to tourists ascending the mountain and reminded them to clean up after themselves. Yazidis fled to the hard, barren top of Mount Sinjar after ISIS attacked their villages in 2014. Crumpled clothing and lonely shoes still litter Mount Sinjar's parched moonscape. Syrian Kurds escaped to the clay-colored cliffs of the Kurd Mountains, outrunning the Turkish army bent on Arabizing northern Syria. Kurds have a proverb, "No friends but the mountains," because Kurdish history is a mosaic of betrayals by outsiders.

By the time I arrived, the mountainous Kurdish region was teeming with foreigners—contractors, non-governmental organization (NGO) workers, oil, gas, mining, and construction engineers, UN personnel, US Department of State (DOS) personnel, DynCorp security personnel, US Special Forces, arms dealers (the one I knew had a gravelly, good-daughter voice, sly eyes, and sleek blond hair), restauranteurs, and English-speaking teachers—transforming the region's urban skin, oxidizing its cities' patinas. The hive of activity was Ankawa, a Christian suburb of Erbil, home to 30,000 people and approximately ninety brothels in 2011. Hotel nightclubs with gun-check door policies; the rundown UN compound, with its private guest list parties; the German Bar, with its huge outdoor beer garden hosting Maypole and Oktoberfest parties; T-bar, home of Monday's Pub Quiz Night and more than its share of gun fights; and the Edge, a beer-soaked dance shack adjacent to the outdoor pool inside the US Consulate General compound were our playgrounds. Wilding through the cracked streets, we'd meet in a haze of watermelon-scented shisha smoke and shake it to outdated club music as if we were dancing at ground zero. Our bodies speaking, we'd bond over a shared nationality or common language, and sex sibilantly as night folded into dawn.

I had been hired by the region's premiere international school, which was part of a global, for-profit education network run by Lebanese administrators. Our cohort of teachers included adventure seekers, pill-poppers, alcoholics, former Peace Corps volunteers, indebted university graduates, Gen-Xers with no savings, unbeautiful losers, one heir to a condom manufacturer's kingdom, and one of Sweden's most notorious sex offenders. (Those two were not friends.) We arrived from the US, the UK, Canada, South Africa, New Zealand, and Lebanon at the end of summer, when the sun-scorched pavement burned with the tang of far-flung sand and sheep dung. Some of us came from big cities of neon and date rape while others came from small towns where Walmart is the center of culture.

We lived in one and two-bedroom apartments on the international school's campus, hallways and stairs connecting our stories to one another. Mostly single, ranging from our mid-twenties to our mid-fifties, and majority female, the teachers sized one another up in the lunchroom cafeteria, hormones raging, as if we, too, had been returned to adolescence, anxious to form tribes in our fantastical new world.

For many of us, it was our first time experiencing such drastic heat. We compared our days without hydrated pees. We traded tricks to relieve constipation and then used our bathrooms aggressively.

We sweated on our apartment balconies as the Lebanese math and science teachers held death match races between bowl-captured camel spiders and water jug-imprisoned scorpions. We cooled ourselves, first at Lake Dukan—until someone took photos of us in our bathing suits and sent them to our director of studies in a shaming email—then at the outdoor pool inside the US Consulate General compound. We devoted ourselves to suntanning as State Department personnel drank cheap white wine like it was going out of style. Walking the hot, dusty streets of the bazaar, we were tsked for holding unopened bottles of water during Ramadan, a time of religious fasting, while behind errant, wind-blown plastic curtains, local young men wolfed down late morning sandwiches in the bazaar's shawarma shops.

Like Alice with her looking-glass poetry, I made sense of the fine print of my new world by holding it up to the mirror of my old one. Gender inequality transcended both. I couldn't conceal my sex, which drew the wrong type of attention. Many of my female colleagues and I were harassed while walking down the street alone, walking down the street with friends, jogging in the early morning, jogging in the early evening, shopping for snacks, shopping for groceries, standing in a bar with friends, standing in the parking lot of a small store, getting into a taxi, getting out of a taxi, accidentally making eye contact, purposefully looking at the ground. Taking up space. Taking in air.

We Western women were always visible, sometimes unattractively so. We were tsked for smoking water pipes at outdoor cafes near the citadel and tsked for showing our bare arms in public as the daytime temperature flirted with 90 degrees. Taxi drivers reached their hands into the back seat, towards our breasts or crotches. Male drivers slapped our butts when they passed us on the Christian city's streets. We were eye-mauled in public, asked to pose for selfies in cafes, asked to pose for selfies at the shiny new Family Mall, asked to pose for selfies emerging from bathroom stalls inside public restrooms.

We learned not to make eye contact with men. We learned not to flinch when passing cars swerved as though to hit us, the drivers' uproarious laughter surfing above their honking horns. We learned to hold our punches when men grabbed our privates in public and learned to hold our tongues when the compound's security guards asked our male friends how we fucked. We learned to comply with late night security guard raids on our apartments to make sure we did not have male guests. We learned that the Lebanese female faculty would be defended when the school's bus drivers acted inappropriately towards them, but the Western female faculty would be blamed.

At some point, we caught on.

Two

Erbil, Kurdistan, Iraq 2011

A Pleasant Addition to Any Classroom

Student Progress Report   Class: 10 Special Track

Class Description: 10 Special Track (10SP) is a pilot program for tenth graders with second to fourth grade literacy levels in English. The administrators of the international school have pledged that these tenth graders will earn the equivalency of an American high school education within the next three years of instruction. To further this aim, 10SP will have 14 50-minute lessons of English per week. Many of the 10SP students are offspring of the political elite.

Teacher: Alex Poppe

Student Name	Grade	Comments
Zoran B.	D+	Zoran is a pleasant addition to any classroom. He has the charisma of a natural leader, just like his famous grandfather, the president of Kurdistan. Most of the male students look up to him because he is wise beyond his seventeen years. Zoran understands that getting good grades is not as important as his last name to guarantee his future success, so he channels his energy into minding his physical health by playing soccer and engaging in various entrepreneurial pursuits, just like his business mogul father, who allegedly snuck 20 million dollars through the local airport and abroad in the company of his children. Zoran organized three friends to chip in $1,000 each to buy the English midterm exam from one of the international school's administrators. Unfortunately, having the exam essay question did not improve his score as he was not able to buy the ability to write cogently and coherently in English.

Daryan B.	F	Daryan is a pleasant addition to any classroom. A mature eighteen-year-old, he rarely disrupts the lessons, preferring to spend class time gazing out the window. Perhaps he is daydreaming about his rite-of-passage weekend in Dubai with his cousin Zoran and their bodyguards. Besides girls, Daryan's other true passion is soccer, which he and his classmates play in the classroom between periods and on the campus quad during their lunch break. Buying Daryan a soccer team would be a better investment in his future rather than forcing his pursuit of higher education. During a chance meeting with his high-level, government minister father, I suggested taking away both of Daryan's iPhones, Facebook, and internet access, as well as limiting his TV time to encourage studying, but these suggestions appear to have gone unheeded.
Afran B.	Inc.	Afran is a pleasant addition to any classroom. I requested he be moved from 10SP into a regular tenth grade class because he is a native speaker of English, having grown up in northern Virginia. He may be failing all his other subjects, but having him sit in 10SP while his classmates write second grade level process essays on how to make buttered toast will not improve Afran's math, biology, or history scores. His rumored substance abuse issue, which precipitated his father's shipping him off to Kurdistan, does not seem to be resolved.
Azwer S.	D	Azwer is a pleasant addition to any classroom...when he comes. He has missed almost as many days as he has attended. As his mother is a public-school teacher, I am surprised she is not more supportive of daily attendance because learning is sequential. Azwer is more excited about his new Kalashnikov rifle than he is about passing tenth grade. He assures me he does not need school because he plans to join the Asayish, the primary intelligence and security agency operating in the Kurdish region.
Destan D.	D	Destan is a pleasant addition to any classroom. Quiet by nature and made more so by his inability to string an entire sentence together in English, he comes to school mostly on time and frequently remembers to bring his books, but sadly not his homework, unlike the majority of his classmates who are sans school books *and* homework. He shares a propensity to stare out the window with Daryan, but given the forlorn look on Destan's face, I can't help but wonder if he is thinking about his father, who was martyred in the Erbil bombings.

Rebin J.	F	Rebin is a pleasant addition to any classroom. An independent thinker, he marches to the beat of his own drum as well as to the imaginary dance music playing inside his head. His sense of rhythm is exceptional: he squirts his cologne in time to music only he can hear so that we all leave the classroom smelling of Calvin Klein's Obsession for Men. He is curious, often asking what different English words, such as moist, mean or inquiring about my other skills, such as if I work out (I had to pull Rebin off another student half his size before he pummeled him) or if I know gymnastics and can do the splits. He is an inventive communicator in that if he doesn't know an English word such as splits, he is able to use finger gestures and words to ask if I know how to spread my legs. With the death of his grandfather, and because his father was long since martyred, this sixteen-year-old has become the leader of one of the most powerful tribes in Kurdistan. I am sure he will lead his people with all the wisdom sixteen years can bestow on any person, especially a person who reads and writes at a third-grade level in English.
Yezda A.	B+	Yezda is a pleasant addition to any classroom, ~~and this time I mean it.~~ At fourteen, she is the youngest of the 10SP cohort but by far the brightest. Despite the fact that puberty is currently punishing her face, and her gangly limbs have declared a riot on her body, she is no shrinking violet. She organized a DAY OF SILENCE, to celebrate the recent April First holiday. During the DAY OF SILENCE no student spoke during class time. Improvising with a touch-the-board game, I wrote lecture concepts on the chalkboard and invited students to touch the part of the lecture they did not understand. Controlled practice exercises followed the same protocol. The lesson was more successful than either the students or I thought it would be. They were so focused on being silent, they might have learned something. I wish every day were April Fools'. Given Yezda's ~~mischievous~~ clever mind, it is my strongest recommendation, (and if I were Yezda's mother I would stand up to my husband and do so) that Yezda's parents move her to a regular track for the eleventh grade, so she can receive the proper TOEFL and SAT exam preparation she will need to attend university abroad. If she stays in the Special Track program, her learning will languish.

Eylo L.	C	Eylo is a pleasant addition to any classroom. He is spirited, or some might say hyperactive, or if we were allowed to use the term ADD, we could treat him for attention deficit disorder, but this network of for-profit schools forbids teachers from using terms such as dyslexia, dysgraphia, and nonverbal learning disabilities to describe student learning hurdles. (This network of schools has also eliminated any mention of the state of Israel in its history/geography textbooks. It has also omitted any content concerning the potential risk of people who are closely related intermarrying from its biology textbooks. Incidentally, there are stipulations that women from a certain Kurdish tribe of the political ruling elite must marry men from the same tribe, usually a cousin.) Eylo reports being very pleased to have a total of three grandmothers from his father's two wives.
Amez K.	D	Amez is a pleasant addition to any classroom. His recent collaboration with other high school film auteurs has yielded a YouTube sensation, a short film featuring the backsides of several teachers writing on the blackboard during classroom instruction. It is hard to believe that his mother, who teaches at another local high school, pushed him to attend this high school rather than her own.
Agrin D	C	Agrin is a ▬▬▬▬▬▬▬ pleasant addition to any classroom. He is undeterred from reaching his goals although his methods remain a bit unorthodox. I can't help but wonder if Agrin was a biter as a child. He has definitely watched a tad too many *Goodfellas* type films. When the history teacher did not let Agrin have his way, Agrin allegedly shoved his desk against his locker, from which he retrieved a gun, and then pointed it at the history teacher's soft back as he wrote on the blackboard. I thought about that story when Agrin got mad at me a few days later and shoved his desk against the lockers. I spent the rest of the class lecturing from the back of the room, standing right next to Agrin's best friend, Destan, in case Agrin wanted to point his gun in my direction. Perhaps students, and not teachers, should have to pass through metal detectors when entering the campus. I wouldn't have believed a student could enter our school with a gun if Agrin hadn't shown me a mobile phone video of his shadow prowling along a school building hallway with a long, barrel-shaped object in his hand. When I asked him what he had been doing on campus after hours, he gave me a *fuhgeddaboudit* response. It is recommended Agrin's parents become more involved in parenting instead of letting that responsibility fall on the shoulders of his underpaid, cannot-afford-to-have-children-of-their-own teachers. On an unrelated note, one of the administrators was allegedly threatened by two gun-brandishing students who came to his office after hours, demanding advanced copies of their upcoming exam.

Since You Arrived, My Heart Stopped Belonging to Me

Like a rat in a cage, I ran circles around the campus in the watery dawn-dusk light. From above, bats printed their shadows on the sidewalks. On a good day, teaching at the international school was navigating a playful obstacle course. A student might inquire if I ate a carb-heavy diet because I was slim everywhere except for my stomach. Another would ask if there was a film version of their latest reading assignment, Shakespeare's *Julius Caesar*, and if so, what was it called. Male sophomores would tell me I should go out with them some time because "I would have so much fun" before they bragged about cyber-stalking me. On bad days, teaching was being thrown off center and smacking up against a padded wall. Sometimes, the students, especially the 10SP cohort, were a walking, talking argument for birth control.

Discipline was a constant issue. Students closely related to the Kurdish president and prime minister knew that the rules didn't apply to them at school as in life, especially since this famous political family had granted the land on which the school was built. I often saw a certain chosen one or two, under the pretext of punishment, joking around with the head disciplinarian, a man I nicknamed Fingernail Rami because he kept his pinky nail very long to signify his job didn't require manual labor.

These famously-named students might have enjoyed the run of the school, but within their fabled family tree there were hierarchies. Two of the family's grandsons explained the importance of being the firstborn son of the first wife in their hoary legacy, illustrating the various lineages in an elaborate family tree they drew on my board. Those sons were usually educated abroad whereas the first sons of second or third wives, or sons born farther down the first wife's line were educated in Kurdistan. Daughters were entirely insignificant.

Motivating the students who were closely related to the political elite required tactics beyond "study well to get into a good college to get a good job" because these students knew their last name was their ticket for success in life. Kurdistan is a tribal culture where *wasta,* the power of connections, is more important than talent, skills, expertise, or experience, and *wasta* is often conferred by the family name. Zoran, the ring leader of 10SP, had the right last name. He scoffed at a TOEFL exam prep reading lesson which outlined the salaries different occupations earn because, as a high schooler, his monthly allowance was bigger than the professional salary of the computer engineer listed in the reading. He wasn't motivated to learn because he knew he would buy my essay exam from a corrupt school administrator, work with a private tutor on a written response, and try to memorize it so he could reproduce it in the exam room.

I didn't know about his evil genius plan until the end of the school year. He basked in criminal glamor as he told me between peels of giggles right before I traded Kurdistan for Germany. I laughed too, out of shock that four high school students had a thousand dollars each to pool together to buy an exam, that a top administrator was corrupt enough to sell it, that Zoran and Destan had still failed it, and that they would tell me everything. At least I understood why Zoran and Destan had had such similar essay responses. What I did know was that Zoran's failing my class would be a stunting humiliation, so I'd periodically request a few moments of his lunch break to appeal to his sense of honor as a future leader. I reminded him he'd need to understand English well enough to process information and decide what was true or false, to make sound decisions for himself and for those who looked up to him. "You don't want others to manipulate you, do you?" I'd ask, benevolently trying to manipulate him into learning. There would be a momentary flicker of interest until cheers from the lunchtime soccer game beckoned from beyond the open classroom window.

For a long time, I was lost on how to get 10SP to care. One day when only Yezda had her homework done, and most of the others didn't have their books, I grabbed a pink highlighter and drew a spikey-haired, smiley face with its tongue sticking out on a blank piece of paper.

"You know what this is?" I asked, holding my drawing up.

Amez laughed. "You're a really good drawer, Miss."

"The word you want, Amez, is artist. This is a drawer." I tapped my desk drawer. "This is a Get Out of Infraction Free card." Infractions were discipline, classroom conduct, or homework violations for which I was supposed to write students up. The administration recorded infractions and sent reports home to parents. "Yezda gets one for having her homework *and* her books, and those of you who don't will get an infraction for each." I walked over to Yezda and put the drawing on her desk.

"No, Miss!" Eylo stood up from his desk.

"Eylo, could you sit back down, please."

Eylo pushed his chair back.

"I'm telling, not asking."

After a beat, Eylo sat.

"Thanks."

"Kick us out, Miss." Zoran said, gleefully.

If 10SP didn't have their homework or their books, I was supposed to send them to Fingernail Rami's office to be punished, but I almost never removed a student from the classroom.

"No, Zoran. If you're not here, you can't learn."

"But Miss, I don't have a pencil." His eyebrows shot up into a drawbridge as his eyes widened.

"Here, you can have one of mine."

"I don't have my notebook," now Zoran's face looked like he was constipated.

"I'll give you some paper, and maybe tomorrow, you'll bring your books, notebooks, pens, and homework to class."

"Miss Alex, what do I do with this?" Yezda held up the Get Out of Infraction Free Card.

"Keep it for the next time you don't have your homework. You give it to me, and you won't get an infraction. Or you could give it to one of these guys now." I swept my hand expansively around the classroom. Eylo whimpered a little. "But it's valuable, so I'd hold on to it if I were you."

All eyes were on Yezda as she carefully slid my hand-drawn, spikey smiley face into her book bag.

"Miss, I want one." Rebin demanded.

"Then earn it."

"How?"

"Anyone can earn one if they do something really, really well."

"But Yezda didn't. She just did her homework. That's not fair," Agrin protested.

"And she brought all her classroom materials. But you're right. Normally that wouldn't be good enough. Everyone else forgot their books, or their homework, or both, so you make her look good. You could even say you helped her earn one." I walked over to my desk.

"Are you really giving us all infractions?" Eylo asked.

"Mm-hmm," I made a big show of writing on a piece of paper. "How many people need something to write with?"

Seven hands wiggled up.

"How many need paper?"

Seven hands stayed in the air.

"This is why you get infractions." I passed out supplies. "How many of you don't have your books?"

Three hands remained up.

"Why? I know you don't bring them home to study."

"I lost mine, Miss," Amez said.

"Then, I guess you'll be at the bookstore during lunch to buy another one before the afternoon's double lesson. I'd hate to have to give you another infraction. For now, if you don't have a book, slide your desk next to someone who does."

"Miss, if we all have our books and papers and pencils for the afternoon, will you erase the infractions?" Zoran, ever the ringleader, negotiated.

"Have your homework done too, without copying off of Yezda, and I'll think about it."

The Get Out of Infraction Free cards caught on as the 10SP students tried to use them in other classes, which made students in my regular classes want them too. When a fellow faculty member I was seeing on the sly connived one from a student, wrapped it around a bottle of wine, and left it on my apartment doorstep to get back in my good graces, I knew the Get Out of Infraction Free card was a winner.

I could offer an afterschool review lesson before a big exam to which no 10SP student would attend. When I had them win a review lesson by collecting three Get Out of Infraction Free cards, they were all in. They'd hustle to earn, beg, or buy a card from another student, or combine cards and ask for a group discount. I'd counter with the vague suggestion that for each friend they brought, they could pick up anther Get Out of Infraction Free card as a reward for sharing, and I'd have most of 10SP sitting in an afterschool review.

Compounding the problem of motivation was that the curriculum assigned by the international school's learning development team in Lebanon had little relevance to the students' cultural or lived experiences. I had to follow it because the learning development team also made the midterm and final exams, which I was not allowed to see beforehand. Kurdish students whose families had survived Anfal, Saddam Hussein's genocidal campaign to wipe out the Kurds, or the Iran-Iraq War, in which two of the 10SP cohort had lost thousands of their tribesmen, did not care about a book recounting Benjamin Franklin's origin story. When they questioned why they had to read it, I could do little but sympathize.

Iraq's present-day education system, born of a dictatorship, eschews critical thinking. Instead, it trains students to memorize and repeat rather than understand and apply. The international school's approach to literature was to test the facts of a book instead of asking the students to imaginatively live the given circumstances of the narrative through guided close reading, text interrogation, and making personal connections to the text. Iraq's approach short circuited the students' ability to develop emotional intelligence.

In a desperate attempt to get the students to care about the big questions literature poses, I adapted script analysis techniques borrowed from my former acting coach Tim Phillips, who had bogarted them from Robert Duvall on the set of *The Lightship*. I pushed 10SP to Sherlock Holmes text titles, speculate on character motivations, imagine what scenes alluded to in the narratives might have been like, and play devil's advocate for choices that characters made, with varying degrees of success. When teaching a whitewashed retelling of the Tuskegee Airmen, I asked 10SP to think about a time when they were treated as less than, and how that felt. To do so was to tiptoe over a lake of cracking ice as their families' memories were twined with Saddam's genocidal campaigns against the Kurds and the Kurd's current fight for independence.

"Like how you gave Yezda that Get Out of Infraction Free card?" asked Rebin.

"I earned it," Yezda glared at Rebin.

"And some of you have earned them since," I pointed out.

"You treat her nicer than us," Rebin didn't back down.

"I treat her equal to you, which may seem elevated since you're not used to seeing women as equals, but that doesn't mean I treat her better."

"You treat her nicer, Miss." Rebin insisted.

"Rebin, how many extra chances do I give you every day? I want you to learn, so I give you what I think you need in order to do so. Did you get an infraction the day Yezda earned her first Get Out of Infraction Free card? No. Did you deserve one? Yes. I could have given you two, so please don't say I treat her better than you."

"Miss, we are men." Rebin stated as though that explained everything.

The bell rang, and I sat down with my forehead on my desk. The push to have them relate literary events to their own lives was a reckoning with my limitations. 10SP continued to approach literature with dread and edges.

When they didn't make me want to tear my hair out, 10SP pricked my maternal instincts, especially when they achieved little victories. If Eylo passed an exam, he'd hold his paper at arm's length as if he expected the passing grade to hop off the page and find its true owner. When Narin, a second-year addition to the Special

Track cohort, received a TOEFL score good enough for acceptance into universities abroad, we hugged each other, bouncing up and down like bunnies drunk on absinthe. My academic quality control manager (think an administrator/disciplinarian/teaching trifecta) told me that when he had opened the email containing Narin's results, he had expected to see a score in the 50s, not the 90s. He had dismissed her potential, yet she had bloomed.

*

One of 10SP's student learning objectives was to write a formal persuasive letter. 10SP groaned predictably when I introduced the topic.

"Whyyyyyyyyyyyyyyyyyy?" Eylo whined, paddling his short legs under his desk, like he was trying to kick the assignment away.

"This is one of the more useful things I can teach you," I said as I walked behind Eylo's desk to put my hand on his shoulder. Although I had to be cautious about touching the male students, a hand on the shoulder could sometimes calm the students, enabling them to focus. "Next year, if you apply to a university abroad, you'll have to write a personal statement. That's a persuasive argument about why they should pick you over someone else. So is a cover letter for a job. Even now, when you ask your parents or me for a special privilege—"

Zoran scoffed.

"You have a better chance of getting it if you make a persuasive argument."

"Like how we should have our lunch hour with our friends?" challenged Yezda. As the only female 10SP student at that time, Yezda would spend her lunch hour sitting off to the side of some cafeteria table, playing a game on her phone. I had been tempted to join her but thought it might cause more problems than it solved.

When 10SP started the school year, their classroom was located in a mostly empty building. Teachers came to them instead of the students moving from room to room. In between classes and during free periods, 10SP was left unsupervised because there weren't any floor monitors in the building. Often, when I entered their classroom, they were playing soccer in it or watching Arabic language music videos on an inexplicably present TV. In the first weeks, I had successfully lobbied to move them, but not the TV, to a building where their peers studied and hall monitors prowled, but 10SP still had their lunch hour with the lower primary grades. They couldn't meet up with their friends for a daytime gossip or play in the upper grades' soccer tournaments, both of which lowered their morale.

"That's a great idea Yezda. I'll teach you how to write a formal persuasive letter, and the assignment will be to write to the director of studies, persuading her to change your lunch hour. Everyone will get an individual grade for their own letter, but if she changes your lunch hour, I will give all of you five extra credit points on the final."

"Ten points, Miss," Rebin pushed.

"Five."

"Seven," he countered.

"Five. Otherwise, we'll write a formal letter of complaint as outlined in your textbook, and you'll keep having lunch with the first graders." I tried to sound like I didn't care which they chose, but I wanted them to fight for something they wanted.

"Miss, I will not need your extra credit. I will get 100!" Rebin proclaimed, his index finger erect in the air, an exclamation point of defiance.

"Good. I want to see that," I said, half-turning to the board to hide my smile. Rebin hadn't passed a single assessment all term.

Turning back around to face them, I announced, "Let's vote. Who wants to write a letter persuading Dr. Kothari to change your lunch hour?"

All their hands went up.

"Great. Let's get started. You'll want to take some notes because you'll each be writing your own version." I explained a formal letter's structure and tone, reminding them not to include shoutouts to Allah, and then taught them what a street address was and how to write one because Kurdistan didn't have a formal postal system. Then, we brainstormed their arguments.

"Miss, they act like we're bad." Zoran's eyes became saucers, his eyebrows hovering above them like launched parentheses.

"What do you mean?" I prompted.

Zoran looked at his classmates. "They keep us away from the other students."

"Like a bad influence." Yezda interjected.

"How does that make you feel?" I asked.

"Bad." Zoran repeated.

"I need higher level vocabulary."

"Like losers." Yezda added.

I took in their downtrodden faces and longed to fold them all under a motherly wing, to protect them from life's ambushes lying in wait. "No slang in a formal letter, please." I corrected softly.

"Alone." Rebin had his eyes on his desk.

"That's a good word, Rebin. Do you remember the prefix 'ex'?"

"Give me an infraction free card, Miss," Rebin demanded.

"It wasn't that good, Rebin." I wrote ex on the board.

"Ex-girlfriend," smirked Daryan, swimming in hormones.

Even I'd heard the rumors that after Daryan had sex with his girlfriend Keje in the backseat of his car, he dumped her. Now, he was chasing after another tenth grader, whom Keje blamed for being dumped. Keje and that girl had gotten into a physical fight, and now the rest of the tenth-grade girls were choosing sides. "Sort of. Daryan, what if I gave everyone a chocolate bar except for you. How would you feel?"

"Bad," Daryan echoed his cousin Zoran.

"Left out, Miss," piped up Yezda.

"Right. Do you know a word that starts with ex that means left out?"

"Excluded." Yezda said.

"Good Yezda." I wrote excluded on the board. "Why is that important for learning?"

"Because we're sad and so we don't care, Miss." Eylo reasoned.

"That's great Eylo. You're saying that moving your lunch hour would improve your learning because you'd feel motivated. Remember, this is a formal letter, so we need to use bigger words than 'sad' and 'we don't care.' Use 'improve student learning' instead of 'do better' when you explain how your reason supports your argument."

Later that week, their letters were hand delivered by a grinning me to a surprised Dr. Kothari. She returned the favor with an impromptu classroom visit a week later, announcing 10SP would be joining the other upper grades' lunch hour at the start of the new term. We erupted in cheers as Dr. Kothari side-eyed me on her way out. Moments like this made me wonder if I should have had children.

A tiny hiccup is that I think babies are fragile, intimidating, shitting machines designed to ruin your clothes with puke and eat up your life with soul-crushing responsibility. Toddlers scream. Kids are only good for running in to get your cigarettes or bowling your turn when you're too buzzed to move. There is nothing more sinister than a tween-aged girl, except a posse of tween-aged girls, prowling the main street in their school uniform skirts and insouciance.

But teens I like. I love how teens' whole world is high stakes: they are either bouncing ecstatically or being fickle little nihilists, ready to slit their wrists. They haven't unlearned how to celebrate life's little joys, and they don't know how to bury their vulnerabilities. They can make an art project out of being sad. They're mentally quick. They'll call you out on your inconsistencies and hold you to account. They're funny. They have fresh takes on the sameness of the world because they haven't lost their capacity for wonder. If I could have birthed a fifteen-year-old, I might have signed up for motherhood.

Cultural norms press many reasons to become a mother. My favorite to hate, especially when it's said to me by someone who went directly from her father's house to her husband's house and never learned how to develop opinions of her own, or by someone who became a decorative accessory in their partner's life instead of discovering the fundamentals and facets of who she is, is that I won't be fulfilled as a woman until I become a mother. Blink. Blink. My stun dies down, and my back goes up as Rice Crispies snap, crackle, and pop beneath my skin. Does being wired without maternal software make a double-X chromosomal less of a woman?

Around the time I was sinking to a Brooklyn floor on my punctured air mattress, looking for answers to life's existential questions the way orphans look for mothers, I stumbled upon theologian Fred Buechner's musings about vocation in his book *Wishful Thinking: A Seeker's ABC*. He posits that we find our true vocation at the point where our deep gladness meets the world's great need. I have found deep gladness and fulfillment in classrooms in Izmir, Kyiv, East Jerusalem, Erbil, and Sulaimaniyah, experiences I probably wouldn't have had if I had married any of the alcoholic or true-hearted or possessive or controlling suitors stuffed into the clown car of men who had proposed to me and had their (or someone else's) child. Unfortunately, there's no parallel control group as we experiment with how to live.

I've heard so many mothers say that motherhood is the most loving, intense relationship they've had, but only a few have confided in me about the deferred dreams it requires or how it can evacuate you. I've heard friends and family members say being a mother makes you fierce, powerful, mature, terrified, cautious, patient, understanding, complete, humble, less self-centered, more responsible, fulfilled. When I think about my own shortcomings—being insecure, resentful, scorekeeping, jealous—I wonder if motherhood would have exacerbated these flaws or smoothed them. If motherhood were a shape, it would be an apeirogon.

There's a short film about a caravan of Central American mothers whose children migrate north to the US, but they never make it. Eventually, the mothers take a bus through small Mexican towns to find out what happened to their *hijos*. They stop in town squares, lay out their children's laminated photos, and tell their stories via bullhorns in the hope that someone will have information. Some of the mothers hold out their child's photo while they explain that their child does not look quite like that anymore because he or she left 15 years ago, but the mother has kept searching. As I watched the film in the blue glow of my laptop, my eyebrows went all funny, and I rocked myself until the craving to buy a dream dress passed. I do not know that kind of sustained, intense, devoted, bottomless love.

The film's title, *Since You Arrived, My Heart Stopped Belonging to Me,* captures the essence of motherhood, which is a weight too heavy for me to carry. If I had become pregnant, my fetus would have been a story growing inside of me: every ambition, accomplishment, and disappointment; every freedom and every rage; every humiliation, every fear, and every shame; every abandonment, every hunger, and every sacrifice; every joy, every sweetness, and every tranquility; every sorrow; every heartbreak; every fight; every possibility, countless like snowflakes. After nine months, I might not have wanted to let my story go.

In a dimly lit apartment in Kurdistan, the one hundred and fifty seconds I held my best friend's newborn were some of the most heart-tranquilizing of my life. Her son, a few days old, seemed impossibly small, impossibly fragile. Innocent and unblemished, he lay in my arms, his closed eyes coin slots above chubby, caramel-colored cheeks. I didn't know how to support his head, nor did I trust myself with the weight of his body. Holding my breath, I waited for someone to take him from me, so terrified was I that I would wreck him.

Three

Erbil, Kurdistan, Iraq 2012

Five Weeks

The students knew. They were the one who told us. Of course, we didn't believe them. Confidently, we told them it was not true. Falteringly, we told them, they must have gotten it wrong. Truthfully, we couldn't comprehend what they were saying. So very little did we know.

*

"You guys are here early."

The students nodded their heads without looking up from their computer screens. I had just walked into the upper grades' English department faculty office, my mind running through the day's tasks ahead. Our office housed a row of computers for students to use to apply to colleges. Normally, the students congregated in our office between or after their classes to gossip about their other teachers or to pry into our personal lives. They were never this focused unless there was an impending deadline.

"Do they have something due?" I asked Renee, my supervisor. She shook her head, her face an egg. Later, I would wonder if she had known what was coming. During my two years working for her, so often had I seen her play dumb to stay ahead.

I walked over to where my student Hawre was sitting, pulling on a thick pelt of side bangs as he read from his computer screen. "What are you working on?" I asked, stooping to nearsightedly peer over his shoulder, careful not to let specific parts of my upper body brush against his back or shoulder.

Hawre half-turned in his seat. "Miss Alex, do you know Mr. Azaan?' his cheeks were flushed.

I paused. Azaan, the international school's IT teacher, had been in my campus apartment a few days earlier, trying to poach me for a job at a Microsoft Future Tech learning hub he was opening in the nearby city of Ankawa. Gossip was rife at the school, and the last thing I wanted was for someone to have seen him entering or exiting my apartment. Azaan had a wife and three kids.

"Sure. He's a colleague." I kept my face very still.

Azaan had told me he was about to take a medical leave from the international school, courtesy of a bogus doctor's note procured with the help of a bribe so he could still earn his teaching salary while he set up the tech hub and got it running. His doctor's note didn't extend to his weekend duties proctoring Test of English as a Foreign Language (TOEFL) exams, for which he earned an extra stipend.

"He was in prison in Sweden." Hawre turned back to the computer, lusty for content.

I wanted to contradict him. How could Azaan have been hired with a prior record? But last term's scandal—involving one of my supervisors, her falsified credentials, and a prescription pill habit, which she may or may not have asked a student's pharmacist father to fill—was a fresh memory.

"For what?" I asked.

"For being one of Sweden's most notorious rapists." Hawre stumbled over the word notorious.

I swore riotously inside my head. "That can't be true."

"It says so here." Hawre pointed to his computer screen, where the day's edition of an online newspaper article with the title, "A Pedophile Got a Job with an Elite School in Iraqi Kurdistan" was open. Ants crawled on the underside of my skin. I stood up and looked down the row of computers where pictures of Azaan with various unfortunate haircuts lidding his gerbil-like facial features popped from monitors. It was a small consolation that Hawre was reading about whatever this was in English.

Hawre read aloud. "'One of Sweden's most notorious rapists who made contact with his victims over the internet'—What does notorious mean?"

"Being famous for something bad." I held my breath, waiting to see if Hawre would ask what rapist meant. When I'd taught his class *The Great Gatsby* the term prior, Hawre asked me what Nick meant when he reported that Gatsby "took what he could get, ravenously and unscrupulously, eventually he took Daisy one still October night, took her because he had no real right to touch her hand." When I explained that Nick meant Gatsby had taken Daisy's virginity, Aryan, another Kurdish student who had been raised in Florida before his family returned to the Kurdish homeland, immediately shot up his hand and asked if I was a virgin as my face lobstered. The school's biology curriculum barely taught sexual reproduction. Just the week before, a gaggle of giggling eleventh grade girls had burst into the office, howling over the Lebanese science teacher's inability to say the letter p in English. "Mr. Edi says benis. Benis!" gasped eleventh-grade Viyan between rifts of laughter. I doubted the curriculum had a unit on consent. I shot Renee a look.

She shuffled over. More tight-lipped than a sphinx, Renee had served in the Canadian Armed Forces, where, allegedly, she had been shot in the line of duty. Her rumored bullet scar and lumbered walk added to her mystique. "What does the article say?" she asked, all naïve and nonchalant.

Hawre continued reading aloud from the screen. "'One

of Sweden's most notorious rapists.' Wait, I read that part." As Hawre's finger trailed a line of text across the screen, I read the fine print on Renee's face and wanted to fashion the school's code of conduct into a baseball bat and smash it against these hallowed walls. The administration must not have learned its lesson from last term's scandal and failed to run thorough background checks on new employees.

"'Was sentenced to ten years in a Swedish prison in 2007 after being convicted of carrying out 58 cases of sexual assault against young girls, including 11 counts of rape.'" Hawre interrupted himself. "What's the difference between assault and rape?"

Gravity got greedier. "Renee?" I volleyed the question to her before escaping down the row of computers, my blood pulsing in my palms. When Azaan had come to my apartment to discuss the job, we'd sat in my living room together. I served us coffee and bottled water. I tried to reconcile the scheming, eye-glass wearing man in a Pillsbury Dough Boy body sitting on my sofa with someone capable of committing close-proximity acts of sexual violence. Azaan wasn't particularly large or strong; were his victims tiny? He must have forged a sense of trust with them. I thought about the smooth way he justified his fraudulent medical leave while he set up his new business and how I had been half-tempted by his job offer.

"Miss Alex, you have to see this." Aland, an eleventh-grade scholarship student with shaken-soda energy and a struggling beard, waved me over. He sat huddled with Rehan, a soft-spoken son from a less-famous line of the region's most famous political family, sharing a pair of earbuds. They were listening to something exciting and revelatory, like desire. When I reached their computer, Aland offered me his earbud while Rehan played a video on YouTube. The three of us hunched together like jewelers around the computer monitor.

The video clip featured a younger, thinner, less bald Azaan defending his crimes to an unseen interviewer for a Swedish TV show. "I like teenagers and I paid them," read the English subtitles. Azaan explained that when he'd arrived in Sweden from his native Iraq, he'd seen a teenage couple making out in a park and thought "anything goes" with women in his newly adopted country. As I listened to Azaan's justification, an invisible hand pressed on my heartbeat. A few months prior, a man walking past me outside a small Kurdish shop had swiftly thrust his hand out, grabbing my mons pubis *hard,* and squeezed it. He retracted his hand like a frog retracts its tongue and walked expertly back to his parked car as my Western, male colleague exited the store. The grabber took off as I unfroze and registered what had just happened. Some colleagues thought the violation was my fault because my knee-length, high-neck dress was sleeveless. Others chalked the assault up to my being foreign.

Othering as a justification for sexual violence is an assaultingly neat argument. Dohuk city cab drivers used it to rationalize attacking female Yazidi survivors of ISIS' genocidal attack on Sinjar and its sex slave markets, figuring that the Yazidi women had already been compromised by ISIS fighters. A government advisor on religious affairs to the Kurdistan Regional Government (KRG) elevated othering to high sparkle. Over watermelon shisha and tequila shots, he mentioned visiting an Ankawa brothel with a group of friends. Right before his lips encircled the plastic, highlighter yellow mouthpiece stuck on the end of the waterpipe, he said he and his friends had shared a thirteen-year-old Arab girl for a few hours. Then, he inhaled luxuriously.

Shock and horror rearranged my face.

He exhaled, and shisha smoke scalloped the edges of our table.

"You seem very pleased with yourself for gang-raping a thirteen-year-old." Sometimes, you have to lash out just to breathe.

"Of course, I am. With a group, it was very cheap."

I flared like a smeared firefly. Clinging to the fact that this advisor on religious affairs lived for shock value, I hoped he was putting me on. In his cocaine-fueled youth, he had fronted a Wham! cover band, singing in London nightclubs, loud and humid, releasing stale gusts of sweat and booze.

"I'm surprised you chose an Arab girl," I prodded.

"Of course, I chose a foreign girl. Who do you think works in the brothels?" He held the water pipe close to his mouth as if he might fellate it.

I changed tactics, trying to break him. "Thirteen is just a little older than your daughter."

The look he shot me left an exit wound.

"Who went first?" I pressed.

"I did, of course."

"Of course."

"Ask Carl the next time you see him. He was there."

My shoulders shuddered with an urge to icky-dance. Carl was his cousin who sometimes joined us for nights out when he was in town from Dubai. "In the room watching?"

"In the next room, waiting his turn."

"That poor girl."

"She enjoyed herself."

"Now I know you're lying."

"For God's sake." His swears sounded like prayers. "I'm facilitating an important service. How else is she going to make a living?"

"She shouldn't be working. She should be in school."

'Idiot!' his voice creaked as his lungs hung onto the harsh, fragrant smoke. "What do you think happened to young Iraqi girls after your country invaded?"

"Miss Alex?" Aland's voice pulled me back into the present. He and Rehan were watching me, waiting for my reaction. From being my students, they knew I was an outspoken advocate of women's rights, an icepack against a bruise.

I gritted my teeth and channeled a gracious Juliette Binoche. "How did you find out about this?" I asked, while inside, I was a snarling dog. How did the students know before the faculty did? In the days to come, the administration would never acknowledge the incident to the faculty, nor did they issue any guidelines on how to talk to our students about it.

"Tofiq's father recognized Mr. Azaan when he dropped Tofiq off for his practice TOEFL last weekend," Aland answered as Rehan left YouTube and surfed the internet. "Then he called the other parents to let them know, and then his father called the school."

Later, when this story was officially told by the school's administration, they would claim to have recognized Azaan and promptly fired him, and then *they* notified all the parents.

"How did Tofiq's father know Azaan?" I asked, my contained temper a few degrees below heatstroke.

"His father saw him on TV in Sweden."

Tofiq and his family had returned to the Kurdish capital from Sweden, part of the diaspora coming home to restart their lives in the region's prosperous safety. If a family had owned land before they fled the violence plaguing Kurdistan from the late 1980s through the early aughts, by the time they returned, that land ownership had made them wealthy. Violence engulfed Iraq, a byproduct of the US invasion, making the Kurdish north, with its large oil and gas reserves, mountains, and more temperate climate, desirable. I taught a pair of Kurdish sisters who had recently returned from Michigan, where their father ran a gas station and convenience store outside a depressed city. Now, they lived in a neo-classical style mansion inside a newly-built gated community.

My eyes swept the office. My female students' faces were contorted and exposed by concentration. Some of them had drawn together in pairs. They talked quietly, their mouths hidden behind hand canopies, their eyes occasionally flicking around the room. Other faces were theaters of implicit emotions, curtained by long, dark hair. A few were twirling their hair as they scrolled and read. Had Azaan slipped into the cracks of their thoughts? If so, were certain moments strobing on and off in their minds like a broken flashlight? Did they blame themselves for enjoying the spotlight of his attention, or were they recasting past events to uproot the seeds of fresh disaster? Were the one or two sitting on their hands, hurting?

A big feeling, numb and shapeless, took over me. I was back in my own suburban high school, with a biology teacher named Mr. Dott, whose black, short-cropped beard and mustache were a reverse image of the patchy baldness stalking the top of his head. He used to interrupt his own lectures to point out how my eyes matched my sweater or comment on their blueness to the class. Heat would creep up my neck and rinse my face red as he lingered over my desk, watching me take notes. I'd ignore the invitations to visit his homeroom after school, written in the upper right-hand corner of my homework assignments, his spidery handwriting creeping across the loose-leaf page. I was fifteen, embarrassed about my budding acne, uncomfortable in my revolting body, and ill-equipped to process adult male attention, which made me feel simultaneously seen and invisible.

My throat found a hum. Handing Aland back his earbud, I told Aland and Rehan that I would see them later and walked out into the mall-lit hall, closing the office door behind me. That door was a portal to a daisy chain of my younger selves who had invested in the transitive nature of trust with varying returns. In high school, two male classmates from highly-respected families, "good kids," had offered me a ride home from a party, and I wound up with my arms pinned behind my back as they took turns feeling me up. The added bonus was the whispered rumors trailing me down my high school's hallways like a lingering smell.

My college-aged virgin-self forgave a boyfriend who had sworn I could drink what I wanted when I was with him because he "was never going to initiate sex with me." His bad boy reputation well-earned, he promised that "if we ever have sex, it will come from you." Upon our post-Christmas break reunion, I stayed back in his apartment because I had to work at my internship the next morning while he went partying and got completely lit. I awoke to his drunkenly pulling the crotch of my underwear aside and trying to insert himself inside me.

There was the thirty-something-year-old me successfully arguing with a date that "we didn't really want to have sex because we didn't really mesh" to get out of his apartment compared to the forty-year-old me who had sex with a date because it was the easiest way to get him out of mine. More than seven years passed since Azaan had been caught and imprisoned. Because individual identity intertwines with sexual identity, were Azaan's victims able to carve into those years and extricate themselves? I hoped his victims were able to rid themselves of his fingerprints. That, as their lives progressed, they didn't settle for fast sex, slow love. That none of them had ended up face-down in some trash-strewn back alley. That they hadn't turned into dust.

*

The day dragged with the weight of newfound knowledge. Finally at home, I turned on my computer and fell down an internet rabbit hole, this one slicked with slime.

Google Search: *A pedophile got a job at an elite school in Kurdistan*

Google Search: *Alexandra Man*

Google Search: *How do I activate Google Translate?*

Google Search: *P3 documentary Alexandramannen*

Google Search: *Books by Katia Wagner*

Google Search: *Wikipedia Alexandramannen*

Google Search: *Alexandramannen Lunarstorm*

Google Search: *Met girls online, ended up with sex abuse*

Google Search: *Eleven years in prison for the Alexandra man*

Google Search: *Eleven years for internet rapist*

Google Search: *Sex offender 'Alexandra' has sentenced reduced*

Google Search: *Alexandra man avoided jail sentence in 2002*

Google Search: *'Internet rapist' enrolled in computer security class*

Google Search: *The Alexandra man gets the right to men's magazines in jail*

Google Search: *The Alexandra man expelled from Sweden last night*

Google Search: *He raped girls – does not pay damages to his victims*

Google Search: *The Alexandra man: a story about the biggest online sex scandal of our time*

Sitting at my kitchen counter, I read how Azaan had posed online as a twenty-five-year-old female model. His profile picture on LunarStorm, a Swedish social networking site for teens, featured a beautiful young woman named Alexandra, sitting on a sofa in a green sweater. From the early to mid-aughts, Azaan befriended teen girls, chatting with them, gaining their trust, and grooming them under the guise of Alexandra. I could imagine his caring texts, punctuated with winky face or blushing kissy face emojis.

I paused, listening to the mournful *Isha* call to prayer, and realized that night had blackened the windows. I got up, stretched, snacked, and returned to my computer, where I found more articles detailing how Azaan/Alexandra encouraged the girls to become models. He suggested they could make money by taking pictures of themselves in various stages of undress, assuring them that the more of their bodies they showed, the more money they would make. They could also send videos of themselves via a webcam. As Azaan/Alexandra gained the teens' trust, he got them to confide their sexual activities, from which he covertly created a database of profiles and added their pictures and videos. Finally, Azaan, still posing as Alexandra, suggested the girls meet her friend FK because he could make them models, and he would pay them for their time. If girls were hesitant to meet FK, Azaan/Alexandra used the pictures and videos they had sent to coerce them.

As FK, Azaan texted and called his victims. He convinced them to come to the city where he lived and booked them tickets to get there. Katie Wagner's book, *The Alexandra Man*, details how Azaan met one girl at the airport with a rose in his mouth. The girls probably went looking for awe but found terror.

When the girls arrived, he took them to parking lots, public toilets, or department store cafes, where he pulled down their pants and made them cry. Some he paid for sex; other he raped, but with all, he never used protection. Some of his victims were virgins. A few of them considered suicide after. One thirteen-year-old became pregnant. The youngest victim was twelve years old, the cusp between milk tooth time and womanhood.

What is a just sentence for rape? For the rape of a minor? Of many minors? In the US, we stigmatize women who are not perfect victims. We often label a rape victim such as Megan Waterman, who was raped by serial predator Rex Heuermann, as a sex worker instead of a mother when she was both. Some of Azaan's victims accepted payments for sexual acts. If he paid an adolescent for a prearranged and rendered service—which did not include intercourse— and then had nonconsensual intercourse with her, was the nonconsensual intercourse an act of rape? Some people may not consider Azaan's acts of sexual violence illegal.

But the Swedish government did. Azaan was sentenced to 11 years in prison and deportation orders after serving his sentence. On appeal, Azaan's punishment was reduced to ten years. Ten Years. 58 victims. 62.9 days per victim, except Azaan served a little more than half his sentence before he was repatriated back to Iraq as a free man. He ended up serving approximately 35 days per victim. Five weeks per girl.

How do you quantify the reverberation of sexual violence across a life?

By chance, I met Sahar, a female Iraqi mental health counselor at a flamenco performance in Cadiz, Spain a few years after I left the international school. We bonded because both of us were reading physical books in the audience before the show started. Originally from Baghdad, Sahar fled Iraq during the Gulf War, eventually making her way to Sweden. She finished her education and coincidentally set up her practice in the same city where Azaan had committed his crimes.

"I can't believe he only got 11 years," I said a few days later as we sunned ourselves at the beach.

"How many years should he have gotten?" Sahar asked, applying oil to her arms, stomach, and legs.

"I don't know, but he attacked over 50 girls. 11 years doesn't seem like enough."

"Long jail sentences are cruel, and they don't help anyone. But in the US, you give out long sentences. Life sentences."

"Doesn't Sweden?'

"They're rare. Other than life, our longest sentence is 18 years."

"That's it?"

"18 years is too long. Prison is supposed to rehabilitate, not punish."

Looking out at the water, I thought about Sahar's use of the word cruel. "What about mass murderers? Or child killers? ISIS? Don't they need to be punished?"

"Spending decades in prison won't make them better people."

"What if they can't change? What if, like Azaan, they don't think they did anything wrong?"

"Anyone can change."

"I go back and forth on if I think everyone can change."

"Do you know the term, moral distance?" Sahar propped herself up on her elbows.

"No."

"It is important to how our prison system is organized. In Sweden, we don't see criminals as that different from ourselves. The people in prisons look pretty much like the people outside of prisons, including the people who make prison policies. We don't see a huge moral distance between those who break the law and those who make the law, so our punishments aren't cruel because theoretically it could be us being punished. Losing your freedom is the punishment, so when people are in prison, we help them. Correctional officers are also social workers. Inmates have access to libraries. They can take university courses and do apprenticeships so they're ready to re-enter society when they get out."

"That's so different from the US."

Sahar made a compelling argument, but I still was unconvinced about Azaan. Even if he had changed, I didn't want him working in an environment filled with teenage girls.

Because Azaan's crime was one of Sweden's biggest cases of online teen sexual exploitation, journalists kept tabs on him for a few years after his trial. Though their news articles were brief, from my internet sleuthing I learned that Azaan had served his sentence at the Norrtälje prison, whose claim to fame is that one Friday night, the staff forgot to lock up 6 inmates, three of whom had been convicted of murderer. With their chance liberty, the inmates baked a chocolate cake and watched TV.

About a year into his sentence, Azaan applied to Computer Engineering, Information Security and Risk Analysis, a distance learning course offered by Mittuniversitetet in Sundsvall. The course would have taught him about surveillance techniques, data corruption, false users, risk analysis techniques, cryptology, firewalls, and other computer security measures to combat cyber threats. In the end, Azaan couldn't take the course due to prison restrictions. He did, however, request access to the men's magazine, *Zoo*, in his cell. Prison officials denied Azaan's request, explaining that the magazine was counterproductive to his treatment because it had pornographic elements. Azaan counter-argued that pictures of women in swimsuits were not pornographic. Otherwise, clothing catalogues such as Ahlen's and Josefsson's would have to be classified as pornographic too. Azaan won.

While Azaan was on his bogus sick leave from our international school, he taught demonstration classes at another school in Erbil under the pretense of applying for a teaching position. That cold November day in my apartment, he told me that he had gone to the other school to see if there were staff or faculty he could poach. Maybe. Or maybe he wanted fresh hunting grounds.

After our school's administration realized who Azaan was, they called the authorities, and within a few days, Azaan disappeared. None of the faculty knew for certain what had happened to him, his wife, or his children. The official story was that the Asayish, Kurdistan's intelligence and special security police, kicked him out of the Kurdish region and back into southern Iraq. We assumed his family went with him. Many faculty members, social Christians from Western democracies, wondered if Azaan had been disappeared by the Asayish or jailed by the Iraqi authorities once he was returned to Baghdad. A few faculty, their lust for justice strong, said they hoped he would be killed. They forgot that Sweden had already punished him.

*

Everyone creates their own fiction. Through a Facebook troll outing Azaan's newly-minted identity, I found Azaan on Instagram. His new name is not that different from his old one. Front and center in Instagram squares, he smiles for the camera, a little older, a little chubbier, a little balder. His profile states he has over 25 years of experience in business management and is highly skilled across the IT spectrum, with "very good strategy-planning experience." The website linked to his Instagram account is for a cyber security firm, where he refers to himself with the title "Prof. Dr" although my Nancy Drewing suggests he never earned a university degree. According to one of his Instagram highlights, sometime in late 2020, he was part of a Microsoft Engineering team in Turkey. There are several posts of him standing in front of flags with his website's logo, handing out what look like plaques of achievement to students of all ages. Lying in bed, I stopped scrolling, set the alarm on my phone, and turned off the light, but not my brain.

In the quiet dark, I reached for my phone. A photo of Azaan

congratulating a mom caused me to shudder. The mom is holding a toddler as Azaan scrunches his frame closer to the child and makes a funny face. I shook my head at photos of him with young adults, captioned with "Team 2021" or "Team 2020." One of his posts titled "Travel is the healthiest addiction," made me sneer. I don't doubt the rehabilitative prowess of Swedish prisons, and if people change, they deserve a fresh start. But real change requires a shift in mindset, and I am not grief proof.

Honor and shame underpin Iraq's societal value system. Men's honor must be protected at all costs, and women are responsible for preserving that honor with their bodies. Attacking a woman's body dishonors her, her husband (if she has one), and her family. She is better off dead if her virginity is violated or her community *suspects* her virginity has been violated because without it intact, she has no value. This is the justification for honor killings. Article 409 of Iraq's Penal Code permits "honor as mitigation for crimes of violence committed against family members," capping the maximum sentence at three years. A judge has discretionary power to shorten the sentence, but this mercy applies only to men. If a woman kills her husband because he has committed adultery, she will be sentenced to the full penalty under the law, which is 15 years. Perpetrators of honor killings typically receive six months, if they are sentenced at all. This is the cultural mindset in which Azaan was raised.

Lava*, buried alive by her brothers in the Kurdish mountains for accepting a ride from a male coworker; Tiba Ali, strangled by her father while she was sleeping in his home in Iraq because she wanted to marry for love; Shnyar Hunar, beaten and burned alive by her intoxicated husband after a domestic dispute in Kurdistan—all justified as honor killings of women in a culture where those who make the rules (men) hold a huge moral distance between themselves and those who must follow the rules (women). Azaan is a product of this culture. He thinks women, especially foreign women with whom he decrees "anything goes," exist for his convenience. In his case, I doubt the Swedish prison system's rehabilitative treatment upended an ingrained, societal value system which holds a woman responsible for safeguarding her honor, her husband's honor, her family's honor, and everybody's reputation with her body yet denies her agency over that body and full personhood.

*Lava asked reporters not to use her last name out of fear for her safety.

Four

Erbil, Kurdistan, Iraq 2012-2013
Leipzig, Germany 2013-2015

Pied Pipers

The SUV bumped over the rutted road, kicking up dust. In the back seat, Silvie's head and mine sailed towards the truck's ceiling as our arms swathed the boxes between us. We bounced back down to our seats, and the boxes, sounding like trash cans in an alley, settled. Silvie and I looked at each other, my left brow cocked, both her nostrils flared. In the front seat, John, a Brit and fellow teacher, drove single-handedly, his other arm slung fatherly across another box. Our SUV was following a white Nissan Frontier, driven by Harun, a Kurdish doctor, its open truck bed heaped with more boxes and full trash bags. Sitting in Harun's passenger seat was Willie, who sported a Sioux Falls Air Force Patrol baseball cap, a watch on each wrist, and a good old boy beer gut.

Harun, John, Silvie, and I had spent the previous evening in Harun's mother's front yard, cleaning, organizing, and packing up dishes, cups, glasses, utensils, kettles, pots, and pans scavenged from the castoffs of aid organizations moving in and out of the Erbil's fluid donor economy. Now, we were on our first aid drop to help refugees recently displaced by the Syrian Civil War. This was do-it-yourself humanitarian aid and relief, the fruition of John's vision and labor. He had seen how emergency aid response got delayed by organizational bureaucracy and wanted to build a non-governmental organization (NGO) free of administrative fat to maximize the use of relief resources. Over the next five years, John's aid organization would grow into a foundation after receiving backing from an angel investor—not Willie, although he was accompanying us to see if he might—made wealthy in the war economy. In the years to come, John's organization would segue from aid and relief into conflict analysis and context, operational mapping, and rapid assessment, advising major regional actors and the UN on conflicts in Iraq, Kurdistan, and Syria.

Accompanying this aid drop, I felt like Alice stepping across the last brook before she is crowned queen. In Iraqi Kurdistan, I had volunteered a few times with a small, local NGO fostering cross-cultural connection and arts education, performing mostly administrative and event planning functions, but I hadn't been in the field. I had spent the previous summer break in East Jerusalem, teaching English to Palestinian at-risk youths for an education, training and development NGO sponsored by the US Department of State, but I didn't consider the classroom, a known, safe place, the field. Today's aid drop was different. There was a sense of ownership because I had helped with the grunt work, and pride because we were delivering humanitarian relief on our own. I was punch drunk on camaraderie and pheromonal with invincibility.

The chalk-dirt road widened—mournful, peaceful—splitting the underdeveloped land, which browned in all directions towards the ever-receding horizon. Banking each side of the road was a single row of cement brick houses devoid of front doors and windows, their gaping black holes like phantom eyes watching our two-truck convoy roll forward in an absence of birdsong. The street scene seemed set behind a sepia-tone view finder; road dust the same color as house brick, both dulled in the watery, January sunlight. There was no grass nor trees; instead, a row of electricity poles lined the newly poured cement street gutters. Pops of color bloomed from the laundry hanging across clotheslines strung in building cavities where there should have been windows.

As the coughs of the SUV and the Nissan truck motors broke

the early morning quiet, tens of anxious men, head-scarved women, and fizzy kids appeared as if from nowhere, running towards our vehicles, the kids whooping and cheering. Some people had on light jackets while others wore plastic slide sandals on their bare feet despite January's chill. They swarmed our vehicles. Opening the truck doors meant hitting people with them, so I cracked my car door only slightly ajar. A barrage of hands and knees breached the hem of space between the car door and the back seat, grabbing at anything in reach. A boy's grimy fingers latched onto the end of the scarf wound around my neck and yanked it toward him, choking me. Self-preservation was stronger than empathy. I batted his and other hands away as I slithered out of the backseat, shutting the door before people could climb in and ransack the SUV. Wide-eyed and frozen, Silvie stayed put in the back seat.

I caught up to John, who had joined Harun in the Nissan's open truck bed. They were trying to get people to form a line before they distributed supplies based on a family's size. A man in a grey hoodie with a lit cigarette dangling from the side of his grizzled lips waved a sheet of A4 paper. Thumbnail-sized photos of his family members and their registration numbers were printed on it. In an effort to coordinate relief services for the thousands of Syrians Kurds streaming across its border, the Kurdistan Regional Government (KRG) encouraged refugees to register, but the situation was so fluid, the data became obsolete before it could be shared among the NGOs working in the region.

We were in a settlement, a piece of land where refugees decide to stay after they have been given permission to do so by the host government. Settlements are not administered by the United Nations High Commissioner for Refugees (UNHCR) and may not receive funding from UNHCR or other big name aid organizations. Instead, displaced people staying in settlements rely on support from local NGOs, community organizations, and sometimes the local government. There were way more people than we had expected, and we didn't have enough supplies to go around.

Outstretched arms fenced in the peninsula of the truck bed—behind them, more people. Guttural shouts dueled children's shrieks, everyone trying to get our attention. Someone tried to pry my gloves off my hands as I was handing out plastic bags of donated items. Harun shouted in Kurdish, trying to tame the chaos as a few teen boys climbed onto the truck bed railings, and the throng of people mushed forward. All of the sudden, the smaller children scampered off. Down the road was Willie, with his arms stretched high above his head, holding Iraqi dinar, the local currency, in his hands. The kids, their open mouths angled up towards Willie as if he were going to feed them, bobbed up and down, reaching for the bills as they waited for him to drop them. Dinars rained down, and the kids jostled one another as they scrambled to pick them up. Smiling, Willie played this game until his pockets were empty. Not all the kids got money.

When the Nissan's truck bed was empty, John called us back to the vehicles. There was a second aid drop point for the boxes in the SUV. Harun got in the driver's seat of Nissan while Willie got behind the wheel of the SUV. Moving like gorillas, John and I ran and climbed onto the back bumper of the SUV because we didn't want to risk opening the doors and having the supplies inside ransacked. Holding on to the roof rack with one hand, I half turned, taking photos on my cell phone with the other. We drove off, exalted and oblivious in the after image, with children chasing after us down the dustbowl road.

We pied pipers.

A Chance Object Fabricates a Life

Duaa raised her fist and paused, the strong April sunlight shadow-puppeting her hand against the wooden front door. Her gummy lips pressed together, rolling inward before she rapped twice. From above, birds were Morse-coding. I stood beside her, clipboard in hand, mute and useless. It was Easter Sunday, 2013, and we had come on behalf of the Agency for Technical Cooperation and Development (ACTED), a French non-governmental organization (NGO), to knock on strangers' doors and count the number of people living behind them.

Dua worked in ACTED's Erbil field office while I was volunteering on a rare Sunday off from the international school. Our task was to find out how many people were living in each apartment and perform a vulnerability assessment, which NGOs use to determine the scope and size of future programming. We had been paired for this assignment by ACTED's country director, Cindy, a Canadian I had met over late night beers at T-Bar. Years prior, the press secretary to Kofi Annan, the former secretary-general of the UN, advised me to go to a conflict zone, find out where the aid folks drank, befriend them, and then offer to volunteer to get my foot in the humanitarian aid sector door.

Duaa knocked again, and the door swung open. Across the threshold stood a bewildered, tattooed, unshowered, twenty-something with a matted whorl of curly hair. He wore counterfeit

Adidas track pants, spelled Addidas, and an untucked T-shirt. In a parallel life, he might have just woken up from a night of clubbing.

Speaking in Arabic, Duaa explained why we were knocking on his door. Kurds in Turkey, Syria, and Armenia speak predominantly the Kurmanji dialect of Kurdish while Iraqi and Iranian Kurds speak the Sorani dialect. The two dialects are basically different languages, each having its own vocabulary, grammar, and alphabet. Speakers of one dialect usually don't understand speakers of the other. The youth before us was a Syrian Kurd while Duaa was an Iraqi Kurd. Most Syrian Kurds speak Arabic because the Kurdish language has been suppressed in Syria since 1955, so Duaa spoke Arabic to this Syrian Kurd in Iraqi Kurdistan.

The young Syrian Kurd listened, his face a theater of quiet emotions. Refugees who didn't have registration numbers might have entered the country illegally and feared being sent back. Stressing that we were from a non-governmental organization that wanted to help, Duaa persuaded him to let us in. Six young men were living in the two-room apartment. They had traveled together from the same village and were loosely related to one another. Resettlement agencies make an effort to keep family members together, especially when several people share one apartment. Some two-room apartments we would visit that day housed two entire families.

Duaa cooed something in Arabic, and we were admitted into a short hallway where several pairs of dusty sneakers and scuffed rubber sandals neatly lined the wall. I hesitated, waiting to see if Duaa would remove her shoes, which she did, so I did too, self-conscious that my bare feet might smell. At least my toothpaste breath was somewhat fresh. We followed our host into the main sitting room, where T-shirts, jeans, and towels hung from nails stuck in three of the room's bare walls. An empty clothesline smiled across the fourth. Suitcases anchored the room's corners while packed duffels skimmed the baseboards, outlining the absence of furniture. Above, a naked lightbulb swung ungenerous light across some maroon floor cushions, where we were invited to sit.

From the adjacent kitchen came the other housemates, all young Syrian Kurds, their bovine eyes curious yet shy about the strange women who had entered their apartment. I wondered if Duaa was worried about her safety or her reputation because we had entered an apartment full of young men, but there was no time to ask. She had already begun the needs assessment, asking them questions in Arabic and translating their answers into English, which I wrote down. Despite not speaking Arabic, I sensed their hesitation about disclosing their registration status. They didn't want to discuss any health issues, but they took the government information pamphlets we had for them.

While Duaa explained how to apply for aid, I peeked through the open doorway separating the sitting room from the kitchen. Bowls of half-eaten cereal dotted the kitchen floor, visited by flies buzzing in through the open, screenless kitchen window. Although we had interrupted their breakfast, they showed no annoyance. Instead, they offered us cigarettes and fresh tea. They had begun to relax, smiling more as they spoke, occasionally making Duaa laugh, creating a painterly tableau. As I accepted a cup of tea, I wondered if one of the young men had brought the cups from home, and a chance object fabricated a life. I imagined a mother, her face a walnut, spooning lemony, garlic-scented rice onto brine-soaked grape leaves before folding them into tight cigars. She packs the stuffed grape leaves and a plastic milk jug refilled with sweetened black tea for her son's journey. I flicked my eyes in the direction of the young men, noting their thinness, the teaspoons of shadows under their eyes.

Cupping my palms over my eyes, I wiped the film of privilege from my imagination with the heel of my hands. These young men's odyssey hadn't been a spring break road trip with friends. Theirs was conflict-driven displacement, with no set return date. Perhaps they feared being forcibly recruited to fight Assad's army, as different militias were rumored of doing, and decided to leave Syria while they still could. Maybe they had been targeted by the current regime and decided to leave before they were disappeared. The viewfinder inside my head refocused: families meeting in a jasmine-scented courtyard to pool their resources and send their boys away. My mind zigzagged across time and space to all the courtyard mothers: glum, melted candles of women, and their daughters, whose smiles curdled when they were left behind to wait. Butterfly lashes blinked back tears as the courtyard emptied, and dust hissed at a sudden touch of rain.

 The cups had probably been donated by another aid organization, the kettle too. I sipped my tea and stole another look inside the kitchen. There weren't any appliances except for the kettle. What would these young men eat tonight and how would they cook it? What about tomorrow? Tea caught on the lump in my throat. I was in northern Iraq by choice, seeking something missing, whereas they were in northern Iraq by necessity, probably missing all they'd left behind when they'd been forced to flee.

Camping

"Come on baby," Cindy encouraged, hunching up over the steering wheel and petting the dash. A spoke of sunlight skidded into her nose ring and sparked in the rearview. "You can do—uhh, can you do it?" She teased the gas pedal, and the Land Cruiser gained on the wind-wrecked mountain, my heart holding as we reached its peak. My stomach bounced to my toes as the SUV slalomed down, and the wheels coasted nonchalantly over the minutes between miles.

Next to Cindy sat Pietro, a slim and smiley northern Italian with a seven-day, fuzzy bear stubble. Behind him and next to me was Jules, a serious, patient Frenchman whose rectangular glasses gave him a professorial air. All three wore functional, multipocketed vests bearing the NGO ACTED's logo and closed-toe work boots. I glanced down at my open-toe, two-inch high, wooden-heeled, John Fluevog clog-type sandals, hockey-sticking the bottom hem of my red jeans and felt like a disaster tourist. Before I got into the SUV, Cindy had offered me a vest, so I'd blend in with the team at check points. I accepted it, grateful for the opportunity to store my Clean & Clear oil absorbing facial blotting tissues and Mac lipstick into the vest's many pockets and ditch my purse.

Earlier that morning, Cindy, the country director for ACTED, an international organization providing humanitarian relief, and her team had picked me up from my compound for the three-hour drive through mud-green mountains molted with browning scrub brush to the Domiz Refugee Camp, set up by the United Nations

High Commissioner for Refugees (UNHCR) and the Kurdistan Regional Government (KRG) to shelter Syrian Kurds fleeing the Syrian Civil War. The camp was designed to house 2,000 families, but a year on, 8,000 families were living in it and around its edges. The overcrowding strained food, water, and sanitation resources, leading to a cholera epidemic. Cindy and her team were going to finish mapping the 150-hectare camp, and I was volunteering for the day to help. Mapping means identifying the coordinates of different points of interest such as community water collection points, public toilets, small shops, and drivable roads into a GPS tracker before marking them on a physical map for future infrastructure improvement projects or social impact programming.

Cindy, Pietro, and Jules had made their careers in the humanitarian aid sector, spoke multiple languages, and had extensive field experience in emergency response areas such as water, sanitation, and hygiene (WASH), conflict resolution, economic development, and relief aid distribution in high conflict zones including Afghanistan, South Sudan, and Pakistan while still in their thirties. I, halfway through my forties, was in awe. In my imagination, they morphed into my own private Heidi, Andrew, and Ken, the three authors of *Emergency Sex and Other Desperate Measures*. Listening to their deployment stories made this the truck ride of a lifetime, so I put my lifetime into the truck ride. Measuring the little I had done in the humanitarian aid space against the North Star of their collective experience, I felt a different kind of privilege to be accompanying them in that SUV.

As we turned onto the access road leading into the camp, a sudden wind scalloped the field grass on either side. Beyond the administrative offices and community buildings lay row upon row of tents, each one stamped with UNHCR in black block letters. Some of the tents were garlanded with white plastic-coated wire while others bore crude patches where they had already torn. Here and there were tents anchored by concrete slabs, an early sign of shelters being fortified for long-term displacement. Adjacent to the backside of many tents were rotund metal cylinders, somewhat bigger than a beer keg, used for water storage. Small satellites dishes sat atop some of the cylinders. Between the tents, T-shirts, towels, and socks hung on thick clotheslines like multi-color pennant flag banners. Large blankets, including a quilt in checkered shades of blue, hung on the barb wired fence marking the camp's outer perimeter. As we drove by, Christiane Amanpour's creamy, hot chocolatey voice reverberated inside my head, asking, "Where have all the parents gone?"

Farther into the camp, Cindy parked the SUV near a series of tents overflowing with brightly-colored plastic housewares, cheap boots, and counterfeit sneakers. These tents were individually-owned small businesses started by refugees so they had money for essentials not provided by the camp. Our slamming car doors broke the late morning quiet. Three women, one pregnant, one holding a toddler on her hip, and the third holding a small toddler in one arm and a larger toddler by the hand, came out from behind a stack of red plastic chairs to stare at us as we exited the SUV. All three, eye-patched in exhaustion, wore hijabs and a mix of traditional and modern clothes. Cindy waved, calling out a greeting in Arabic as we gathered at the back of the truck, and the women continued to stare.

Cindy passed out the GPS trackers and divided us into two teams before assigning sectors for us to map. Due to some recent issues of sexual violence, single men had been moved to their own section of the camp, which was still under construction, while single women were housed in the family section, the largest in the camp. Jules and I paired up to finish mapping the larger part of the family section while Pietro and Cindy took the smaller part and the men's section. Jules taught me how to use the GPS tracker, which looked like a cross between a black, old-timey cell phone and a TV remote control attached to a lanyard. I slipped it round my neck, and off we went.

Despite the cholera outbreak, children ran barefoot along rivulets of water flowing from the latrines to serenade us with *Hello* and *What is your name* and then scampered off before we could answer. In the autumn mud, they brandished toy rifles, stopping to gape at our funny gadgets. Cheeks flushed rosy, curls matted to foreheads, eyes backlit with delight, and no school to attend, they ran circles around our progress as the sun gained on the sky. Dodging their mayhem, Jules stepped in what looked like molten chocolate cake batter outside latrine 8, in hectare 32. For a second, I froze and stood like a chess piece.

"It's probably just mud," I said, trying to smear tactful goo over his predicament. My hand dug into my vest pocket for a fistful of facial oil blotting sheets, a dilettante's triumphant Girl Scout moment. "Here." I offered as I took a few steps towards him, holding my breath against a waft of funky decay.

Jules shook his head and scrapped his boot against the ground. Surveying the results, he took the oil blotting sheets and leaned on my shoulder to clean the rest as best he could. Now, I understood his choice of footwear.

In hectare 46, a line of men and boys extended from the barber shop and wrapped around a dry goods store, portable shop 18. Another boy with no need to shave paraded up and down the line, selling cups of sweet black tea from a tray hanging around his neck. My stomach rumbled. As we marked the barber's location in the GPS tracker, the fathers called out to us, offering us packages of snack cakes and penny candies in celebration of Eid al-Adha. No wonder so many men were waiting for the barber, lest their beards look homeless. Jules and I each took a candy before Jules offered iodine tablets from one of his vest pockets in return, explaining why and how to use them. Jules placed the tablets directly into the men's hands instead of holding them up high and letting them helicopter down so the men could scramble to catch them.

"Alex? What are you doing here?"

I turned, startled to hear my name. In front of me was Renas, a male staff member from the international school. What I was doing in a refugee camp was a quicksand question. For reasons I never understood, the faculty were not supposed to volunteer with other organizations while employed at the international school. "Hi Renas. I'm helping some friends today," I responded, keeping it vague. "What are you doing here?"

"My aunt and cousins are living here. I came to see them for Eid."

Above, a few clouds flushed a blue canvas of sky. "That's so nice of you," I said, trying to cover my surprise. I didn't realize anyone on our staff had family living in a refugee camp.

"Thank you for being here," he said. "I can't believe an American teacher would come on a day off from school."

"Don't thank me," I said, feeling the blood of my eager, awful aspiration to connect with something bigger than myself scribble my cheeks. If I hadn't been volunteering, I might have been sunning myself on my apartment balcony, reading a book on my Kindle app, steps away from reliable plumbing I didn't have to share. Meanwhile, thousands of people endured a daily lack of sanitation in the camp, and his family members were among them. "It's great to see you, but I should find my friend. *Jazhnt Piroz*, Renas," I said, butchering "Happy Eid" in the Sorani dialect of Kurdish.

With my bladder as tight as a fist, we finished mapping our

hectares and rejoined Cindy and Pietro. The *muezzin* sounded the late afternoon call to prayer as the sun slid behind the mountains with a click of cold. Given the cholera outbreak, we decided to eat at a restaurant in a nearby city instead of supporting one of the restaurants inside the camp. I silently cheered at not having to use a camp latrine before a pang of guilt sliced me.

Over chicken kebabs and Turkish beers, we discussed the situation in the camp. Cindy worried that the tents not fortified with concrete foundations would flood with the upcoming rains. Jules thought cholera would continue plaguing the camp unless the sanitation system in the latrines was improved. Pietro commented that the men's section was not yet livable and wondered when more schools would be built to accommodate all the children in the camp. I said little, thinking about the word camp.

I have never been camping. Before this trip to Domiz, my idea of camping was staying in a tent for a few days to unplug from city chaos and reconnect with nature. Since I love cities, hate bugs, and like to keep nature at arm's length, camping does not appeal. In Charlie Hailey's book, *Campsite: Architectures of Duration and Place*, Hailey defines camping as an intentional or unintentional, temporary occupation of space. He observes that campsites are places of "locality and foreignness, mobility and fixity, temporality and permanence, and public domesticity," concluding that camping is a way of making a home, and our homes are constantly evolving.

Much of what Hailey observes in campsites is true of refugee camps. By definition, refugees are people who cross a national border, so they are foreigners in their new localities. Fleeing war, persecution, and violence makes them mobile, which ends when they reach a camp because many camps restrict refugees' movement outside of them. If refugees cannot be integrated into the host community or be resettled in a third country, they are fixed in the camp, a displaced person's personal *No Exit*. Although refugee camps are designed to be temporary, the World Bank cites the average stay in a refugee camp as 17 years despite temporary water taps and bussed in food. Tents evolve into homes as they become fortified with concrete, lined with blankets, and fitted with satellite dishes for internet access. Living within the sound-permeating cloth walls of a tent, sharing latrines with strangers, and cooking out in the open or communally puts domestic life on display.

As I tuned back into the conversation, Pietro was talking about an upcoming tent distribution close to the Syrian–Turkish border. Although impossible due to my teaching schedule, I longed to accompany him. Leaning back in my chair, I realized that as much as I wanted to join their world, I was too in love with indoor plumbing and too tied to dry clean only dresses and antique jewelry to work in humanitarian aid programming as they did. I was much more effective in the classroom, where I focused on my students' empowerment and critical thinking, instead of in the field, trying to be someone I was not. I drained the last of my bottle, fished out my phone, and asked if I could take their photo. I was desperate to capture the moment even though I knew it had already gone.

Decamping

A funnel of black smoke billowed up from the ground, fanning high above the electrical wires canopying the street. Along the cracked pavement, men gathered in clusters to watch. Leaning forward until my nose almost touched the laptop screen, I scanned the *Reuters'* photo, looking for familiar faces. ISIS had just detonated a car bomb outside the US Consulate compound in Erbil, on a street lined with cafes and counterfeit alcohol shops, both of which were popular with foreigners. If I hadn't traded northern Iraq for Leipzig, Germany and a shot at domestic bliss seventeen months prior, I'd probably have been there, picking up a few bottles of wine or having brunch inside the compound's Mexican restaurant.

Sitting in my Leipzig kitchen, my mind hopscotched through a mental photo album of memories and landed in Erbil. There was a candlelight, first-date dinner on Erbil's US Consulate compound, organized by a security contractor, seventeen years my junior. I had met him at my first consulate compound party, back when the DynCorp security personnel could attend the compound's pool parties in nothing more than their swim trunks and a smile. For our date, he borrowed a table from the Edge bar, hauled it up to the rooftop of one of the compound's residential buildings, and hired an off-duty waiter from the compound's Mexican restaurant to serve us. There were the countless Friday afternoons spent suntanning and gossiping with fellow teachers at the Edge's outdoor pool as a State Department bureaucrat got drunk enough to suggest a partner swap. I remembered how I'd bring a backpack full of fresh fruit and boxes of cake mix to my contractor boyfriend and his roommate, who liked to bake. How that roommate would run lookout so my boyfriend and I could disappear inside their apartment where civilians were not allowed for an hour or so of privacy and freedom.

The kitchen's milk carton-colored walls seemed to close in on me. With needles in my belly, I messaged my ex, hoping he had not been on guard duty when the attack happened. Thankfully, he and his friends on the base were okay although three people on the street had been killed and over a dozen others had been wounded. I jumped onto Facebook Messenger to check in with old friends and students. A crew of faculty had been at a nearby café when the bomb went off and got caught up in the mayhem of smoke and gunfire. They were scared but otherwise unharmed. As heart and smile emojis from my former students pinged my messenger app, my old life echoed back to me like a half-remembered song. Part of me wanted to return.

When I first moved to Leipzig, I radiated, vivid with possibility, but now I was shellacked, stuck and numb. Although I am not brave, I longed for the intimacy of risk and the fellowship of adventurers. Kurdistan's cities teemed with journalists, politicians, think tank researchers, humanitarian aid workers, special forces, independent contractors, and thrill seekers, crackling and ready to meet the world head on. I wanted to be near them, if only on the sidelines.

In northern Iraq, the specter of war and geopolitical intrigue hovered over the fringes of daily life, making classroom conversations and pub powwows pop with exceptionality. One of my Kurdish students who was a grandson of Kurdistan's then president sketched out Kurdistan's chummy yet covert relationship with Israel using euphemisms and his eyebrows to add texture and intrigue. Later, a Pakistani colleague colored in the details, outlining how Israel provided training to the Peshmerga, Kurdistan's security forces, in exchange for oil, some of which Kurdistan illegally siphoned out of Iraqi pipelines in a practice known as bunkering. On the faculty bus to Ankawa, I'd hear scraps of conversation about how top Kurdish leaders were arming and training the Syrian Kurds because the Syrian Civil War presented *the* opportunity for Kurds to unite and form an independent nation. On pub quiz nights, whispers swirled like cigarette smoke around a contractor who looked like Forest Whitaker and was rumored to be one of Idi Amin's illegitimate sons.

In Leipzig's social scene, people debated the Greek debt crisis, intensified by the specter of a third EU bailout. They argued whether Germany should continue accepting refugees as anti-immigrant sentiments intensified. Besides my adjunct teaching gig at a technical university, most of my students were business professionals of relative affluence taking night time English classes for fun. Our chats revolved around family life, travel, and German culture. Inwardly, I kicked myself for having chosen safe domesticity over unpredictable intensity.

My German partner resented my desire to return to Kurdistan, disdainful of what had once attracted him to me. "If I told you I needed to climb to the roof of that building and jump off, would you let me?" he asked one Sunday as we strolled down a city street awakening to spring.

"It's not my place to *let* you do anything."

"You wouldn't try to stop me because it was dangerous?"

There was a razor of cold in a sudden breeze.

"If you felt like you really, really needed to do it, I would respect your decision. I'd watch."

"You'd what?"

"As support. I wouldn't like it, but I'd make myself stay and watch."

"I can't believe you wouldn't stop me."

Our armors clanking, he stormed ahead.

As my nomadic stirrings harried the fissures in my relationship, I chanced upon an online article in the *New York Times* about the fates of 23 ISIS hostages being held in Syria. I was reading the line chart showing who had been taken, how long they had been held or were still being held, and if they had been ransomed or executed, when my eyes stumbled over a familiar name. My shout was half animal, half guttural. My hands steepled over my nose and mouth, and I watched a fly cling to the kitchen window until my breathing slowed. A few months after we mapped the Domiz Refugee Camp, Pietro was taken by ISIS while surveying a refugee camp near the Syrian-Turkish border.

Sitting at my computer on the kitchen table, the walls of our Leipzig apartment dissolved into a wave of dull, low mountains waiting sullenly for rain. Ghost echoes of children shrieking between rows of dirt brown tents drowned out the early morning music program my partner listened to while he showered. Closing my eyes, I inhaled the pungent fugue of sunbaked earth and dung. I saw Cindy, Pietro, and Jules walking up the main road of the Domiz camp, and me, a day traveler in the task of emergency response, following behind.

My partner entered the kitchen wearing a white bath towel around his waist, trailing the scent of his cypress and sea fennel shower gel. "What's wrong?"

A bead of water dripped from his hair and slid down his neck. How could I adequately explain the roil of fear, shock, worry, and regret waving through me? It was ineffable, like the way heat and cold can both burn. "A guy I know from Iraq was taken by ISIS."

"I'm so glad you're not there anymore." He chuffed my shoulder as he glided through the wariness between us to pick up the cup of coffee that I had made for him. Then, he glided back to the bedroom to get dressed.

I'm not, I thought as I reached out to Cindy on Facebook, needing to connect with someone who would understand. In a series of voice messages, she recounted how she had also been in the field that day but luckily had been safe. There was an endless jagged breath before she said four of her colleagues had not. In the next message, her voice broke as she explained that they had been killed, and a fifth, who had been taken with Pietro, had just been beheaded. Her third message quietly explained that Pietro had been released. The Italian government most likely had paid his ransom. In her last message, she said she was now back in Canada, working as an asylum case manager.

In a sundown of feeling, I scoured the internet. I read how after a year in captivity, Pietro received a proof-of-life question: what was the color of the bedroom walls in his mother's house? He knew then he would be released.

A year of psychological and physical torture. Weeks of solitary confinement. Long stretches of time without a shower. Sometimes denied food or water. I recalled the lilting musicality of Pietro's Italian accent, how his dimples elongated and all his teeth showed when he smiled, and wondered how much of that Pietro had survived. Two photos in a subsequent BBC article show a wary man, hands shoved in his pockets, shoulders curled inward as though not to take up space. His eyes seem to plead with the camera. His smile is a grimace, trailing its way to pain.

Closing my computer in the after image of orange jumpsuits, I listened to the swish of early morning traffic outside the window, and surfing above it, the dog whistle of restlessness. Over the last eighteen months, I thought I had been making a home with my partner, but I had been unintentionally camping. I thought about how he had wanted to get engaged on New Year's Eve, and I hadn't. How I had no desire to live permanently in Leipzig, where he shared custody of his daughter. How our domesticity would often turn public: our shouting voices would penetrate the floorboards as we argued like we meant it. How humiliated I felt curling up in the corridor outside our front door when he had locked me out. How my singular experiences in Iraq rendered me more foreign than did my US nationality in Germany. How often I felt stuck in the no man's land of wanting to make the relationship work and not wanting to admit that it didn't. There was no more denying the structural vulnerability of our camp. I needed my home to evolve. Within weeks, I decamped, renting a room from a woman who made great fruit cobblers on Sunday mornings. In that liminal space between mobility and fixity I stayed, until a teaching opportunity at a university in Sulaimaniyah, Kurdistan presented itself, and I could return to northern Iraq and feel useful again.

Five

Sulaimaniyah, Kurdistan, Iraq 2015

Board Porn

"Do I need to draw this on the board?" My voice swaggered.

A few heads bobbed up and down as one of the male engineering students yelled "Yes!" from the back row.

Hamburger stains formed under my armpits. I had just offered to draw a threesome on a whiteboard in a classroom at a university in northern Iraq, where faculty could be fired if someone accused them of being publicly drunk. This was also my first lecture with these students. Resolved not to lose this game of chicken, I picked up a marker and drew boldly. Hangman-like stick figure porn emerged. I turned back to the class and, channeling a Stepford Wife, asked in butter-velvet voice, "Now, who can describe Ceremony Night?" as blood scribbled my cheeks.

I had recently been hired by the university to teach English as a Foreign Language (EFL) in its professional development institute. A few weeks after the start of the term, I was asked to take over a literature class in the undergraduate program in addition to my EFL course load. Inheriting a syllabus and an in-progress course, I furiously read the assigned books, *The Handmaid's Tale* and *The World's Wife*, starting off barely one step ahead of the students.

The Handmaid's Tale is Margaret Atwood's feminist dystopian novel that takes on patriarchy, authoritarianism, and theocracy. In Kurdistan, girls can be shot dead by male family members with impunity, justified as honor killings. Carol Ann Duffy's poetry collection, *The World's Wife*, retells well-known, male-dominated stories from the female perspective, keeping the women front and center. In Duffy's world, girls rule whereas in our city, a local, single woman could not rent an apartment by herself, and any whiff of female impropriety could ruin a family's reputation because tribal connections thread the fabric of society. Would the seven female and seventeen male freshmen and sophomores taking this class be receptive to the ideas in these books? Most of them still lived at home and were at that age of recognizing parental and cultural contradictions. At the very least, I wanted both the men and the women to realize they could improvise on the life they had been raised to live.

Many of the university's students came from affluent, politically connected families, so Iraq's future would be shaped by them. How did the seven women sitting before me see themselves in that future when their culture didn't always hold space for them? How could I create a dialogue which encouraged the seventeen men to view women as equals? I wanted all the students, but especially the young women, to learn how to show up for themselves because they recognized their own value. I wanted them to seize life's opportunities, not skip over excitement and land in fear.

Margaret Atwood set a ground rule for herself while creating the dystopian world of *The Handmaid's Tale*. She would not include anything that hadn't already happened in some other place, and any technology referenced in the book must already exist in the real world. She set *The Handmaid's Tale* in the Republic of Gilead, the former United States. In the wake of a global fertility crisis, Christian fundamentalists gain control of the military and assassinate the president and most members of Congress. Once they have taken over the government, they institute a totalitarian theocracy based on Puritan beliefs and the Old Testament. One tenant of Gilead proclaims that women are subservient to men, and their sole purpose is to bear and raise children. Handmaids, women who are still able to conceive, are indoctrinated into the beliefs of Gilead at the Rachel and Leah Re-Education Center. When they finish training, they are assigned to live with elite couples who are barren. Once a month on Ceremony Night, when a handmaid is most likely to conceive, she has forced intercourse/ritualized sex with her Commander, the husband of the elite couple, after he reads the Bible aloud to his household. Handmaids can be placed in up to three different households over the course of two years. If they do not conceive a child in those two years, handmaids are declared Unwomen and sent off to the Colonies, a place contaminated by pollution and radioactive waste, to die. Gilead's handmaid system doesn't acknowledge that male infertility exists.

Ceremony Night is based on an Old Testament biblical story. Jacob's favorite wife (he had two), Rachel, urges Jacob to have sex with her handmaid, Bilhah, because Rachel believes she is barren. In *The Handmaid's Tale*, on Ceremony Night, the Commander has sex with his handmaid, Offred, while she lies in a cradle of Serena Joy's legs, and Serena Joy holds the handmaid's hands. Serena Joy is the Commander's wife.

Although this was an undergraduate class, probably half of the students read in English at a tenth-grade level. First, I needed to check the students' understanding of the assigned reading. By asking relevant questions, I could assess whether the students had read the required chapters at all (or just the SparkNotes) or had read and understood the text on a literal, figurative, thematic, and hopefully philosophical level.

Standing in front of my stick figure threesome, I called a name at random. "Hana?"

Sitting in the first row, the eyes of a fragile waif wearing a hijab bulged.

I took a step forward as she recoiled as far as back her seat allowed. "Let me guess." I smiled like a dentist's receptionist. "You're Hana. Can you describe the Ceremony Night?"

Hana's hands flipped up, palms out in front of her chest as if to ward off evil.

"Who's in the room?" I prompted.

"Serena Joy, Offred, and The Commander." Hana's voice was a susurration. Standing right in front of her, I could barely hear her. As I stooped a little to hear her better, her chair scraped backwards along the classroom floor.

"That's right." I straightened before I repeated her answer to make sure everyone could hear it. "How are they arranged?" I gestured to my drawing.

Hana's shoulders shuddered.

I pointed to the long-haired stick figure in the middle. "This is Offred. Who is she lying on?"

"Serena Joy." Hana's mouth moved but almost no sound came out.

"Serena Joy," I repeated loudly. "Why are all three of them in the room?" I tapped the board.

Everyone had become hard of listening.

I was transported to watching *9 1/2 Weeks* on the VCR in my parents' den on a college visit home. My dad walked in and, unfamiliar with the film, sat down to watch it with me, which proved to be one of the longest, stickiest, most silent, *am I breathing?* 90 minutes of my life. I decided to put Hana out of her misery. "They are in the room so Offred and the Commander can have sex in order to produce a baby." I spoke so quickly my words ran together like a pack of dogs. I called on another student. "Tela?" A girl with a short avant-garde haircut gave me eye contact. Promising. "What makes the sex bearable for Offred?"

"The Commander and Offred don't kiss. It's forbidden. And

she keeps her eyes closed," answered Tela, with near native English fluency.

I smelt an avid reader.

I was unsure how much of the sex connotations I should explain. The syllabus had been built around feminism, patriarchy, and authoritarianism, to which sexual agency is intrinsic. I also wanted the students to understand the nuances of Atwood's writing so they could relish her sly humor as a reward for grappling with the larger questions of patriarchy and authoritarianism within the story. Plus, explaining the sex jokes would probably keep the students reading, or at least listening. Since Tela had brought up the closed eyes, I went for it. "In the novel, there are several references to women keeping their eyes closed during sex. Why?"

Everyone studied their blank notebook pages.

I was surprised. Students shared ISIS beheading videos at the ready, yet discussing a fictional sex scene in a piece of literature rendered them mute.

"First wave feminism focused on voting and property rights for women. Second wave feminism, which lasted from the 1960s to the 1980s and therefore would have influenced Margaret Atwood's writings, broadened feminism's focus to include sexuality, family, and reproductive rights." I had never sounded this professorial. I am the kind of teacher who invites a student to the front of the class to take a swing at me as a demonstrative engagement before I teach the passive voice. (The student *hit* the teacher versus the teacher *was hit* by the student.)

Twenty-four pairs of deer-in-the-headlights eyes stared back at me. Nobody was writing anything down. I probably sounded like Charlie Brown's teacher to them.

"Before second wave feminism, women—especially nice girls—" I put "nice girls" in air quote marks while I hated myself for doing so, "weren't supposed to enjoy sex. The purpose of sex was to have children, just like in The Gilead Republic of Atwood's novel. That's what the 'Close your eyes and think of England' line in the novel refers to. The payoff for having to go through sex, which women were supposed to endure rather than enjoy, is having a child...if you like children." Heat rose from behind my ears. "But second wave feminism said, wait, no, women can have sex for pleasure, just like men do. That sex isn't just about having children, and women deserve to be, uh, satisfied during ah, ah a sexual experience, as men are, and, uuuuuaahhhmmm, they are not bad or shameful for wanting to enjoy it."

My face was a Flamin' Hot Cheeto, and Hana wouldn't look in my direction. The moment rivaled that of standing in front of your entire junior high with a giant period stain on your jeans. On the upside, I had woken up the back row of male engineering students who took this class because it was required.

At that moment, the risk of humiliation was a huge spider web hanging over our classroom, a net of mortification waiting to ensnare. Our embarrassment about discussing sex was short-circuiting our ability to connect to one another. Because learning anything is relational, the students needed to lower their guards, trust me, and trust one another in order to absorb all they could from this class. They needed to embrace their awkwardness and surrender to the intimacy of risk. If they did, they'd be open to the possibility of connection, which is where life's real learning takes place.

I crossed to the front of my desk and sat on a corner to lessen the height difference between the students and me. "Look, I know I'm blushing. Can we all agree we might talk about some things that will make us feel uncomfortable? I'm embarrassed. You're embarrassed. Let's get over ourselves and accept we're going to be embarrassed sometimes."

There seemed to be a collective exhale. From somewhere came the soft scratches of pencils moving across paper as a few students started taking notes. I hoped they weren't just drawing stick figure threesomes.

"So, the line about keeping her eyes closed is making fun of the pre-feminist notion that women should 'do their duty' and let men have them in order to make babies." I paused. "Look at that. My own language is patriarchal although not as colorful as Atwood's. Men *have* women. Why don't women have men?"

"Because men have all the power," offered a teddy bear of a young man. He looked almost sad as he said it.

"Good. What's your name?"

He pushed his eyeglasses up the bridge of his nose as he answered, "Hasan."

Hasan's hair was cut in a high fade, and he was built like a US college football quarterback. He was ten years old when the US invaded Iraq in 2003. After US soldiers killed 17 Iraqis in Falluja in the early months of the war, resistance fighters in Hasan's hometown of Heet started planting bombs for coalition forces at night and then collecting the unexploded ones in the morning so that the people living there would not get hurt. The resistance fighters also beheaded or shot anyone who worked with the Americans, videotaping their operations and leaving them on compact discs around the city. Some mornings, Hasan awoke to streets littered with compact discs. Other mornings, the streets were littered with dead bodies and bullets. Hasan and his friends used to collect gunpowder from the spent bullet cartridges glittering the streets and light it on fire for fun.

Once, an American convoy of four Humvees and a tank stopped at an intersection 40 meters from Hasan's middle school. In a breath, half of the tank lay in a ditch while the other half seemingly evaporated. From the Humvees came a hail of fire while the resistance fighters, holding their fire, yelled to the teachers that they had one minute to pull their students from the schoolyard back inside the building. The soldier's minute stretched—a helter-skelter melee in mute—before the resistance fighters launched rocket-propelled grenades. The next day, middle schoolers found hands, brains and helmets around the schoolyard.

Hasan told me this story when he was no longer my student, one of the countless young Iraqi adults who had seen red tracers blush a night sky. The violence which many of the students had already experienced juxtaposed to their shyness about asking a girl out for coffee pinched my heart. These novice adults had had childhoods scored and scarred by war, making them wiser in some ways than I would ever be, yet naïve about cultivating romantic relationships and reticent about discussing how men and women inhabit space and time together.

"How can we change that men have all the power?" I prompted, hoping the students would start making text-to-self and text-to-world connections, deepening their engagement with Atwood's words. "Although I realize that not all of you may want to."

There were a few chuckles. In the front row, Hana cracked a smile.

"It seems like an impossible task, right? Like, where do you start?"

Some heads nodded.

"How many of your moms went to university?"

A few hands went up.

"See that?" I gestured out to the classroom. "Look how many hands are up. In one of my adult English classes, half of the students' mothers didn't finish high school. Change is already happening."

Now switched on, the students powered back to life.

Pressing my advantage, I continued. "Education readies people to question injustice. That's why women were banned from reading and writing in Gilead. Taking this class, reading this book, learning about feminism and authoritarianism—these are other steps. It's just like the theme of ignoring versus ignorance that runs throughout the novel. Ignoring is complicity. Ignorance has a cure. You can choose to ignore injustice or you can choose to bear witness and change what you don't like."

"Miss Alex, what if I don't want to be a feminist?" Rojan, a female student with a Gucci handbag, asked. She would be engaged before the end of her sophomore year.

"You don't have to be. Although feminism is a political ideology, it is also a personal choice," I paused. Feminism was a category to smudge. "How many of you want to be mothers?" All the female students' hands went up. "Do you think being a mother means you can't be a feminist?"

Lots of heads bobbed up and down.

"You can be both. Or either. Or neither. During our lives, we learn how to balance the contradictions within ourselves. By the way, feminists can make great mothers because they instill in their daughters a sense of self-worth. Some of the women in this classroom may choose never to work outside the home. That doesn't mean you aren't a feminist, or you shouldn't be educated. Everyone needs to know how to take in information and decide for yourself what is true or false in order to make the best decisions for yourselves, your families, and your communities. That's one reason education is so powerful, and why some governments restrict the opportunity to be educated for some or all people." This wasn't the time to point out that Iraq's education system, devised by a dictator, eschewed critical thinking and problem solving in favor of memorization and recitation.

The next week, I showed the students a TED Talk with Sarah Jones performing part of her one woman show *Sell/Buy/Date*, set in a dystopian future as *The Handmaid's Tale* is. The play takes place in a far future lecture hall where a teacher leads a class discussion based on five interviewees commenting on sex work in 2016: an old Jewish woman who thinks pornography has taken the tenderness and love out of sex; a sex positive feminist college student of privilege who sees sex work as empowering although she does not participate in it and plans to become a lawyer; a black immigrant domestic care giver who turns to sex work to find economic empowerment but does not find sex work liberating; a 63-year-old Irish nun-turned-prostitute who thinks sex work keeps young women lost in their own lives; and a male Wharton MBA grad student standing outside a strip club on the night of his own bachelor party. He doesn't count stripping as working in the sex industry.

There was a lot to unpack from the TED Talk. Few young people openly dated in Kurdistan in 2015. The Irish nun-turned-prostitute character said she had never been asked who she wanted to be. She was told, and in her late middle-aged life, she still didn't know who she was. Societal-prescribed gender roles had prevented her from determining who she wanted to become. When I asked the students to name the roles women were assigned in either *The Handmaid's Tale* or *Sell/Buy/Date*, "nun," "prostitute," "handmaid," "wife," "stripper," Unwoman," and "daughter" littered the board.

"In which role in these works of fiction does a woman act for herself?" I asked.

Tela was the first to see it. "The Unwoman."

Her perception felt like the first day of summer. "That's right. Who are the Unwomen?"

The students swung into participation.

"Divorced women."

"Feminists."

"Protestors."

"Failed handmaids."

"Lesbians."

"You're doing great. What do a lot of the Unwomen have in common?"

"They try to be free," Hasan offered. "So they get sent to the Colonies, where there's radioactive stuff, and they die."

"Women thinking for themselves scare men," Tela riffed.

"Lesbians hate men," challenged Ali, a student who would go on to plagiarize his end-of-term essay.

"Feminists hate men," yelled Wael, one of the engineers grapevining the back row.

"Not true," I confiscated the conversation before either Ali or Wael could hurt themselves with it. "Being a lesbian means you prefer women to men sexually, not that you hate men. Also, not all feminists hate men. Some think women are better than men—"

Ali slapped the top of his desk before he turned in his seat to egg on the engineers, my own private peanut gallery. They chuckled in a complicated key.

"But that is just as dangerous as thinking men are better than women," I continued talking as I walked to the back of the room. Nothing kept these students on their toes like standing behind them while lecturing. "At its core, feminism argues for equality within the political, social, and financial aspects of society."

The class swayed away from commotion.

"Now, I'm really going to blow your minds. Men can be feminists, too."

Their collective laughter was the whistling flare before fireworks unstitch a night sky.

"You think that's funny?" I smiled to myself, mentally noting to bring in a video about stay-at-home German fathers changing diapers on paternity leave. "Just you wait."

All Together Now, "Penis!"

Adapting a character finding exercise from my actor training days at Circle in the Square Theater School, I asked the students to work in pairs and, using characters from *The Handmaid's Tale*, create a scene that didn't appear in the book. I wanted the students to experience the novel's characters as three-dimensional people, living within societal and cultural constructs that somewhat paralleled their own. Also, Kurdish culture is steeped in oral storytelling through song and poetry, so I figured the exercise would appeal to the students, especially those struggling to read in English. I hoped the assignment would ease the countless manholes of awkwardness we fell into during classroom discussions about the Madonna-whore complex, Playboy bunnies, masturbation, orgasms, faking orgasms, pleasure, homosexuality, and pornography in order to fully understand the text.

Surprising me, the students dove in, ready to ham it up. Playing on their size differences, Hasan and a small Jordanian named Haider created a scene between The Commander and his chauffeur Nick, who is having an affair with the Commander's handmaid. Their creative play was fraught with cat and mouse tension as the Commander tried to trick Nick into admitting the affair. Tela, playing Serena Joy, the Commander's Wife, and Hana, playing the handmaid Offred, enacted a scene after the first Ceremony Night, in which the two women plan out a nursery. Tela's face, oscillating between jealousy and joy, humanized Serena Joy while Hana's natural fragility captured Offred's trauma. Watching them work, I was reminded of a Margaret Atwood quote: "Those who lack power always see more than they say." Lava, a student with rowdy green eyes and a penchant for missing class to attend gender rights conferences, and Rekan, a dead ringer for Brazilian actor Wagner Moura of Pablo Escobar fame, created a poignant scene where Offred finds her husband Luke in the future, after too much time has passed for them to belong to each other again.

Acting out their scenes bloomed into deeper discussions of patriarchy and male competition, gender violence, and how totalitarian systems destroy lives before the students trellised into tangents on environmental degradation and manufactured news. From relating *The Handmaid's Tale* to their world, the students organically debated Iran's meddling in Iraq, the US occupation of Iraq, ISIS, ISIS and Yazidi women (The year prior, ISIS had stormed Sinjar Mountain, the ancestral homeland of the Yazidis, killing most of the men and sexually enslaving the women.), and women's rights. Then, on a Friday afternoon, as clouds like swan bellies floated across a swimming pool-colored sky, a father shot his teenage daughter in a local park to restore his family's honor.

The theme for the following Sunday's lecture was women's control of their own bodies. Over the clickety-clack of heels in the hallway surfed a flotsam of voices speaking Kurdish, which stopped at the classroom's threshold. The students filed in, their faces drained of health. They lumbered passed me, the floor tiles never so intriguing. As Tela slapped a notebook on her desk, it detonated with dog-eared handouts, which slipped onto the floor.

I walked over and picked them up. "My bad. I should hole punch these before I hand them out to you guys." I gave the papers to her before hesitantly patting her shoulder. She mumbled thank you.

I decided to address the elephant in the classroom and asked,

"Does anyone want to talk about what happened over the weekend?" My question sailed above a brooding sea of bent heads, smacked into the back wall, and sunk to the ground.

"This is a safe space if anyone wants to say anything," I prodded. Since many of the students were locals, I wondered if anyone knew the victim or her family.

The students responded with shrugged shoulders and shaken heads but no actual words.

I blundered into the day's discussion points. "The assigned reading highlights how childbearing is a measure of female worth." I felt fraudulent. Honor killings underscore how women don't own their lives, how little value their lives are perceived to have. "What's your reaction to that?"

The students turtled further inward.

I rewarded academic diligence by calling on the smartest and consistently most prepared student to rescue this class discussion from a looming black hole. "Tela?"

She squinted at me like a cowboy smoker before responding, "At least the women in Gilead are celebrated for having daughters and not just sons."

Standing in the front of the classroom, I saw Ali roll his eyes and wanted to handprint his face. To steady myself, I pictured him in ten years, balding and shaped like a potato. "How else do the people of Gilead measure female worth?"

"They don't," Rekan finally said.

"Offred gets to go out with the Commander," Hasan observed.

"It's not like she could say no," countered Tela.

"She wanted to go," Rekan argued.

"To break up the boredom," Lava challenged.

"Or to look for her husband," whispered Hana.

Their responses petered out, so I asked, "Hasan, how is going out with the Commander a measure of Offred's worth?"

"It's a privilege to go out. It means she's special."

"But it puts her in danger if she's caught." Tela argued. 'Only her, not him."

"That's a great point, Tela." I thought about the young woman recently murdered in the park. Had some "privilege" resulted in her being murdered? "Being given a privilege could be a recognition of worth, but sometimes it's also a risk. How do you measure your own worth?"

"Grades," Haider offered.

"That's Miss Alex measuring our worth," joked Rekan.

"I measure how well you satisfy student learning objectives, not your worth," I corrected and then added, "Measuring your own worth according to your own values helps you know who you are. The nun-turned-prostitute in *Sell/Buy/Date* said that prescribing roles for women keeps them from finding out who they are." My breath caught in my lungs. Had that girl in the park paid with her own life for daring to discover who she was? I drank a bit of water. "In *The Handmaid's Tale*, females are identified as mothers, wives, or daughters. Like most of the women in this classroom, I've played only one of those roles—"

"Why aren't you married, Miss?" Ali interrupted, his words rolling thick and menacing off his tongue.

Sighing theatrically, I responded, "Students tell me it's because I can't cook rice," and gloated as the class's laughter silenced him. "But most of you might be all three: son or daughter, husband or wife, father or mother. Who's to say who among us, at the end of our journeys, will have discovered our true selves? My hope for all of you is that you listen to your inner voice and find out for yourselves who you are."

Some students would not get the chance. Within the next

year, a few would be lost as they tried to smuggle themselves into Europe. Some would not be allowed to return to this university in Kurdistan after President Masoud Barzani's failed Kurdish independence referendum and Iraq's subsequent closure of Kurdistan's borders. Others would have to assume new familial responsibilities as fathers, uncles, or brothers were killed or wounded in Turkey's attacks on the Kurds in Kobane following President Trump's withdrawal of US troops in northern Syria.

As set out in the course syllabus, the companion text to *The Handmaid's Tale* was *The World's Wife*, Carol Ann Duffy's poetry collection highlighting the ill treatment of women through historical, biblical, mythical, and fictional contexts. Ms. Duffy plucks women out of supporting roles and puts their inner voices center stage. Her poems retell well-known stories from a woman's point of view, illuminating new truths: It's better to marry a beast than a prince, as shown in the poem "Mrs. Beast;" women don't pine away while waiting for their men to return, exemplified in the poem "Penelope;" and women don't always want to be saved as in the poem "Eurydice."

Because the students were afraid of poetry, I started with thematic questions related to their prior knowledge or experience to spark a personal connection to the poem under discussion. Then I reviewed the source material on which the poem was based. Lastly, we mined the poem for its insights on gender, patriarchy, and feminism.

Most male students in the class hated the collection, dismissing the poems because Ms. Duffy is a lesbian, which prompted a spirited discussion about reader bias through a filter of homophobia. On campus, some male students gleefully complained that the university's Kurdish, feminist rockstar professor and I "hated [their] penises," but in class, they looked a bit scared. Women in this poetry collection seduce, kill, manipulate, consolidate power, and find artistic fulfillment. In other words, they act like men.

Male classroom discomfort reached an all-time high when I unpacked the poem, "Mrs. Aesop," which is based on John and Lorena Bobbit, a married couple who became internationally famous after Lorena cut off John's penis while he was sleeping. She claimed he had raped and abused her for years. On the night of her arrest, she told the police that John was selfish because he always orgasmed but never waited for her to orgasm when they had sex. Eventually John was acquitted of rape while Lorena was acquitted of assault by reason of insanity. John's penis was reattached, and he became a porn star while Lorena became an advocate for domestic violence victims. Carol Ann Duffy re-envisions *Aesop's Fables* from the perspective of Mrs. Aesop, who wants less clichéd stories and more passion in her marriage. She threatens to castrate her husband by cutting off his tail, his metaphorical manhood, to bring an end to his boring, moralizing tales.

After explaining countless cringe-inducing topics such as masturbation, orgasms, and menstruation with relative nonchalance during classroom discussions, a penis got me in the end. Perhaps I am not as much of a feminist as I thought. To explain the poem, "Mrs. Aesop," I needed to lay out the infamy of the Bobbits. The first time I said "penis" during the lecture, my face was a tomato. I giggled—another humiliation. As the lecturer and alleged adult in the classroom, I was supposed to set the tone. Instead, I had regressed to the maturity of a thirteen-year-old boy relishing fart humor. "Ok, time to get over ourselves and own our embarrassment," I announced. "On the count of three, we are all going to say 'penis.' Ready?"

The students looked back at me, game with uncertainty.

I held my hands like a conductor. "Okay. On the count of

three." I waited for the now familiar bob of heads several weeks of our embracing the intimacy of risk had earned.

I nodded my head, too. "All together now. One, two, three... penis!" I shouted, my hands slicing the air. They chimed in, creating a natural rhythm of joyful noise. Once the embarrassment was out of our systems, I resumed the lecture. The students kept a tally of how many times I said the word 'penis' (nine times), which, without fail, compelled snickering at each utterance. Explaining the poem's line "cut off his tail to stop his tale" imploded the class's concentration just as the bell rang.

I taught these students for ten of their thirteen-week semester with the goal of piquing their curiosity and widening their perspectives so they could molt out of themselves and fly. Hana never did find her voice. Hasan and Tela formed a friendship with each other and me, which lasted beyond their graduation. Hasan started his career in the humanitarian aid sector, eventually segueing to a recruitment job at a university in Baghdad while he worked on developing a virtual reality project of his own. Meanwhile, his parents tried to arrange a marriage for him. Tela, always an avid reader and compelling writer, took a creative position at a local marketing agency before moving on to better job opportunities in Erbil. I lost track of Lava after she went on to a master's program in the Czech Republic. Rekan became "the man of his house" upon his parents' divorce. At the end of the term, he thanked me for teaching his section, saying, "Now, when I hear peoples' stories, I wonder what their experiences are. I want to know them. I want to know what they think."

Six

Sulaimaniayh, Kurdistan, Iraq 2017

"Men Grow Old and Have Bored or Stupid Sons."
-Herbert Butler

The body leaves us long after the self.

For months, former Iraqi President Jalal Talabani lay dying in a German hospital. Better known by the Kurdish moniker Mam Jalal, meaning Uncle Jalal, President Talabani was a founder of the Patriotic Union of Kurdistan (PUK), one of the two major political parties in Kurdistan. He was deeply revered in our city because he had challenged President Masoud Barzani's tribalism and his party's corruption. Masoud Barzani was the leader of the other major political party, the Kurdistan Democratic Party (KDP) and the President of the Kurdistan Region of Iraq (KRI). I had taught many of Masoud Barzani's grandsons at the international school in Erbil. Both political parties had their own military forces called the Peshmerga, which reported to separate leadership.

Many of my adult students in the professional development institute viscerally disliked President Barzani because they felt he had betrayed the Kurds. In the mid-1990s, the PUK and the KDP fought a bloody civil war. Despite Saddam Hussein ordering the execution of thousands of Barzani men and boys in 1983 (One of my former students who is a grandson of Masoud Barzani sent a driver to take another teacher and me from the international school in Erbil to the Barzan heartland, where a cemetery for these victims is located.), Masoud Barzani asked Saddam to help the KDP fight the PUK during the Kurdish Civil War. This was about eight years after Saddam Hussein had committed genocide against the Kurds during the Anfal campaign in 1988.

Azade, a social worker taking English classes in the professional development institute, recalled hiding in a cellar with the rest of her family during the poison gas attacks, trying not to breathe. Her classmate Ziryan was a teen, climbing over slick, icy mountains with his mother and younger brother into Iran while his father stayed behind to fight. Rivin, another classmate who joked that he had a lot of guns because he liked to match them to his shoes, boasted that although his grandfather still owned land in Erbil, Rivin couldn't visit it because he risked being arrested or killed due to "deeds done" by the family during the civil war.

During the war on ISIS, the Peshmerga prevented ISIS from taking Kirkuk. With this victory, the Kurdistan Regional Government (KRG) gained control over Kirkuk's oil reserves, which account for 40% of Iraq's total oil reserves. The KRG could now export Kirkuk's oil through its pipeline to Turkey, bypassing Baghdad. There was a tiny, not tiny, hiccup. The 2005 Iraqi Constitution states that oil revenues Kurdistan receives from selling crude sourced in the Kurdish region are supposed to go to Baghdad. In return, the KRG receives 17% of Iraq's total federal oil reserve revenues, which includes money from both the Iraqi and Kurdish fields. Iraq's central government threatened to cut the KRG out of all federal oil revenues if the KRG sold oil on its own, but the KRG thought that oil discovered in the Kurdish region after it had become an autonomous region belonged only to Kurdistan. The KRG snuck oil abroad through Israel to Malta in decoy ships to avoid detection. Fed up, Baghdad cut off the 17% budget allocation to the KRG, which funded 80% of the KRG's budget in 2014.

Later that year, the price of oil started falling, partly from ISIS selling cheap crude pumped from Syria's and southern Iraq's oil fields through intermediaries to the international market.

Without the budget allocation from Baghdad and with the price of oil low, the KRG couldn't pay public sector salaries. Sulaimaniyah was hit hard as over 60% of its workers were employed in the public sector. Sometimes, my adult students would go three or four months without getting paid, and when salaries were distributed, they were often only a third or half of what was owed. At first, people were patient, relying on the tribal network underpinning Kurdish culture to survive. If a person didn't get his salary one month, someone else in his extended family probably did, and family members would share, covering one another depending on who had gotten paid.

As budget shortfalls continued through 2015 and into 2016, there were electricity blackouts and water shortages, but not looting, not even when the police went on strike. There were street protests. Azade, Rivin, and Sara, another student and a journalist who'd had her life threatened for reporting on gender-based violence, declared they'd rather forgo their income than let the Barzani government win. They believed that the KDP had stolen oil revenue that belonged to the entire Kurdish region, not just the KDP, anchored in Erbil. They wanted Barzani to honor the no-competition *muhasasa* agreements made with Mam Jalal after the 2003 invasion. The *muhasasa* system is a quota-based system used to divvy up government positions and resources in Iraq. After the 2003 invasion, Masoud and Mam Jalal agreed to a no-competition *muhasasa*, deciding that government positions and resource revenues would be split equally between the two parties to present a united front and show the international community that Kurdistan was stable and secure for investment. Azade, Rivin, and

Sara believed that the KDP had violated the *muhasasa* agreement and not split oil revenues equally with the PUK.

As Mam Jalal faced corporeal demise, President Masoud Barzani faced a political one. According to the Kurdish constitution, his eight-year presidential term was to have ended in 2013, but he struck a deal with the PUK to extend it for two more years. In 2015, he extended his term limits again, arguing he should stay in power while the Peshmerga led the fight against ISIS after the Iraqi forces had collapsed. Opposition parties objected, and the Kurdish Parliament was suspended in 2015. Through a controversial court decision, President Barzani stayed in power.

In September 2017, as Mam Jalal clung to life in Germany, President Barzani reactivated the Kurdish Parliament to vote through the September 25th referendum on independence, President Barzani's final stab at cementing his legacy. The referendum vote was a powder keg because it included the disputed territory of oil-rich Kirkuk, which the Iraqi central government claimed as its own. An independent Kurdistan would need the oil revenues from Kirkuk to fund itself, but Kirkuk lies 20 miles outside the Kurdish region's borders. It is home to Arabs, Turkmen, and Christians, many of whom did not want to be part of an independent Kurdistan. The Iraqi government condemned the independence referendum, calling the vote unconstitutional and the inclusion of Kirkuk illegal.

International support for the referendum was a balloon which could not stay aloft. The US and its EU partners were committed to a One Iraq policy, meaning they didn't want to see the country carved into thirds: a Kurdish north, a Sunni middle, and a Shia south. Turkey and Iran were not in favor of the Kurdish referendum, officially because they thought it would reverse gains made in the fight against ISIS, and unofficially because they did not want their own Kurdish minority populations to rise up.

    Whispers that the Kurdish airspace was going to close sent the Kurdish elite scurrying out of the country. From our balcony, we watched white Toyota Land Cruisers filled with men in dark suits carrying big guns escort the families of PUK officials from the building caddy corner to ours. The day after the referendum, as the sun set in a haiku of color, my roommate, JJ, uncorked and booked a flight to Istanbul, preparing to do a runner. History being made was a sewing needle stitching me to the city. Over adult beverages on our balcony, we weighed the possibility of war between Iraq and Kurdistan as a moonlit cat crept along the silvered parking lot. We discussed exit strategies, but neither of us knew the university's evacuation plan, only that there allegedly was one. When we asked what it was, we were told that we couldn't be told for our safety. Pushing for details was like pushing Jell-O up a big hill with a tiny spoon.

    Back when I lived in Erbil, I volunteered with a start-up NGO to bring relief aid to two makeshift refugee settlements. Because the need was greater than our supplies, we couldn't open the truck's rear doors between aid drops. When we did, people would reach in and try to grab what they could before we closed the doors. Instead, another volunteer and I climbed onto the truck's back bumper and, clutching a roof rack for support, rode standing on the bumper over a hand-me-down road to the second settlement. Hanging onto the roof rack with one hand, I snapped photos on my cell phone with the other. As I pocketed my phone and went to grasp the roof rack with both hands, the driver accelerated and hit a ditch. I lost my grip and belly-flopped onto the dirt road. Skidding on my front, my vanity arched my upper back, keeping my head and neck high. All I could think was, *I have to save my teeth*. As I road-rashed the flesh from my public bone to my belly-button and busted both my pinky fingers, I remember thinking, *this will be okay*. Waiting for the post-referendum fallout felt like that. And drinking helped. In the end, the weight of student loan debt convinced JJ to eat his Istanbul flight and stay. In our apartment, rumors and prayers set up house in a daily routine.

Bedtime prayers sometimes work like birthday candles. On September 29, four days after the non-binding and legally questionable referendum vote in which Kurds overwhelmingly chose independence, the Iraqi government closed Kurdistan's airspace, taking control of its two international airports. Iraqi troops began running drills along Kurdistan's borders with Turkey and Iran. Border crossings between Iraq and Iran were closed, and Iraq clamped down on Kurdistan's oil exports, further decimating Kurdistan's economy. Kurdish banks were put under sanctions. Supermarket shelves started to empty. The Kurdish region was effectively sealed shut, and we were stuck within it. Green-black oil and blood in salty light; these were the colors inside my disco anxiety. I taxied to the liquor store to stock up on tequila.

Stardust and Voodoo

Eight days after the referendum vote, our city gave a silent shriek of grief. Mam Jalal had died.

We had just started the school term. I had traded teaching in the university's professional development institute for teaching in its academic preparatory program, swapping adult students for eighteen- to twenty-two-year-olds. As word of Mam Jalal's passing swept through the corridors, glisten-eyed students got up and left their classrooms, spreading in all directions like freed lab mice, wildly scattering into parts unknown. A senior faculty member cancelled his classes, dismissing students as our department director sent an email instructing us to continue teaching. When we tried to enforce the attendance policy, the students accused us of insensitivity. Daintily dabbing her nostrils with a tissue to save her strict lipstick, my student Rojin explained, "Miss Alex, you no understand. You Americans don't to care your president," before she packed up her designer book bag and left.

She was right. Most of us Westerners didn't comprehend what Mam Jalal meant to people in this city. In Sulaimaniyah, billboards featuring Mam Jalal greeted passing drivers on many major roads, and his framed photo was proudly displayed in government offices. Because Kurdish culture is tribal, many people in our city claimed a genealogical connection to the great man.

Within a few hours, the university capitulated to grief's demands and closed the campus for the rest of the week to allow for mourning. Most businesses closed too. Faculty gathered at my neighbor Luke's apartment, where he made faux margaritas by blending borrowed tequila with the last of his Carrefour's citron sherbet.

The next morning, as locals gathered on a soccer field near a mosque in our neighborhood to grieve, I ventured outside. History was being made, but I stood on the outside of it, watching with my nose pressed up to the metaphorical glass. A mix of Peshmerga and Asayish, the intelligence arm of the Kurdish security forces, stood shoulder to shoulder, pillaring the street in front of our compound. Arish, a former student from Azade's cohort, stood as lean as a letter opener in a fresh Asayish uniform. Although ambivalent in my opinion of the Asayish, I was happy to see Arish had found employment. He was a university graduate when he took my adult English course, caught in a spiral of joblessness and inertia caused by the falling oil prices and Kurdistan's budget shortfall. When he was my student, Arish always came to class dressed in business casual or a suit and tie despite his home having about four hours of daily electricity and sometimes no hot water in the cold winter weather. I understood his need to be well-groomed as a strategy to maintain his motivation while daily life conspired to beat him down. Arish acknowledged me with a tip of his chin before he said something to his commander and then broke from the line to escort me across the street, from where I continued on to the mosque.

Eyeing the throngs of people filling the intersection, I took a shortcut up a side street, unprepared for the gray way memories came at me. The ghost echoes of my hurried footsteps as I tried to ditch a driver following me back from the supermarket one night. He kept switching sides of the street as I did, pulling ahead, parking, and waiting until I confronted him, screaming "Fire!" (which no one understood because I yelled it in English) to make him drive away. I thought about the Syrian Kurd who ran the corner dry cleaner and whom my German ex-boyfriend tried to sponsor so he could get himself and his family out of Kurdistan. Opposite the dry cleaner was the fruit seller, his teeth cracked with use. He always popped extra pieces of fruit in my bag but overcharged the Asian sex workers living in our compound because he disapproved of their livelihood. Under my breath, I cursed ornately.

The sidewalks trimming the mosque were thronged with mourners. Following a line of women, I moved through chaos to enter the mosque, grateful I had grabbed a scarf to put over my head as I left home. I realized I had never been in a mosque filled only with women before because I had always entered mosques as a tourist. The parts open to the public were used only by men for prayer. I had taken a discreet place in the back when I saw Solin, one of my students from the previous term, standing in a row of women who physically resembled one another. Solin was a baby feminist who proudly declared her father happy his wife had given him five daughters and no sons. As soon as Solin spotted me, she came over to hug me hello and thank me for coming. The darkish Nike swooshes under her eyes made me feel fraudulent. I had come out of curiosity and a fleeting hope of political celebrity sightings, not with the intention of offering support. Before I could object, Solin was pulling me over to meet her family. I felt a languid stirring of outsider shyness but managed to deliver a well-used smile.

After the recommended time limit governing social interactions, I left Solin's family and returned to my corner in the back, trying not to attract attention, which, as the only Westerner in the mosque, was impossible. When the row of women I was standing in moved, I followed a woman whose face was latticed with long wrinkles. We exited the mosque and entered the funeral receiving line outside to offer condolences. There stood Azade, her mouth a twisted rictus, as she nodded and shook hands. In a weightless moment, I flashed back to our many classroom hours together. Her bourbon-barrel laugh, her barrel-sized generosity. She always exuded life like a lamp giving off light. Now, her face was a skin balloon with eye holes. Suddenly, the undamaged blue sky above seemed offensive.

When Azade spotted me, I expected her to put her right hand over her heart and half bow as is a customary Kurdish greeting for people physically far from one another. Instead, she pulled me in, her palm kissing my scalp. When we hugged, her tears wet my cheek, a grossly cozy intimacy. I hadn't known Azade was so closely related to Mam Jalal. Now, her indignation against Masoud Barzani's violation of the *muhasasa* agreement made a different kind of sense. For her, the betrayal was personal not economic, yet while she was my student, she never let her *wasta* show.

"Alex, how did you know?" Her voice was as frank as wind.

The line was backing up behind me.

"I didn't. I am so sorry."

The snake of people behind me hissed me forward. As I walked home, the sky had the decency to flush with clouds. I longed for rain, the kind that pocks and pits glassy surfaces.

*

We lived at the whim of stardust and voodoo.

Mam Jalal had been dead for 13 days. Our second full week of instruction had just begun. I was still learning the students' names and building the kind of trust that allows you to color outside the lines.

The students were returning from a break between class sessions. Unless a student was a parent, I enforced our department's no cell phone policy and required my students to deposit their phones in shoe bags hanging on the wall next to the classroom door. Just as

I was about to close the door to start the lesson, Diyako, a student with sideburns like waterfalls, rushed past our classroom door, down the hall, and out the building's entrance. Suddenly, several phones hanging in shoe bags started buzzing or ringing, rivaling those still in people's pockets. (Some students had multiple phones so they could surrender a decoy and keep another discreetly close for cheating.) There was a volley of shouty Kurdish words and a few long glares at the Arab students sitting in the classroom.

"Guys! English."

Some students went for their phones.

"Please sit down. Can someone tell me what's going on?"

The day before, the Iraqi government had issued a deadline for the Kurdish Peshmerga to withdraw from Kirkuk. President Masoud Barzani, believing the US would intervene on Kurdistan's behalf if the Iraqi army attacked the Peshmerga, didn't budge from the oil-rich province. After all, the Peshmerga had been instrumental in driving ISIS from Mosul three months earlier and had helped US forces, Iraqi forces, and the Shiite Popular Mobilization Forces (PMF) liberate Hawija, ISIS's last bastion in northern Iraq, just two weeks earlier. Masoud miscalculated. As night knitted over the region like an eyeless mask, Iraqi forces began military operations to retake Kirkuk.

Mohammed, a student with the makings of a good kind of hustler and a second phone in his hand, explained that Diyako had received a text saying his father had been killed, and Mohammed needed to go find him. No amount of teacher training could have prepared me for this moment.

"You can get your phones," I moved to block the doorway and buy myself some time, "but I need all of you to stay in the classroom." Several students had family members who were part-time Peshmerga. A few students were from Kirkuk. Still others were

Iraqi Arabs, who were sometimes bullied or ostracized on campus. Everyone was emotionally raw, still grieving the loss of Mam Jalal or anxious about border closures and troop build-ups.

Mohammed said something in Kurdish to his posse of friends, and three young men started packing up their things. "You can't keep us here," Mohammed yelled, his voice a downed powerline snapping on the pavement. No doubt he was picturing his own father, lifeless on the ground.

"You're right. But I would like you to calm down first."

Mohammed sneered before he rushed out of the classroom, followed by his three friends.

"Please wait here for me to return," I implored the rest of the students before I ran after Mohammed and his friends, catching the four young men in the campus parking lot. Breaking teacher-student protocol, I grabbed Mohammed's arm. "Mohammed, please come back to the classroom."

"Mark me absent. I don't care," he yelled, rage and grief cutting him from inside out.

"Mohammed, this isn't about attendance. I don't want you driving when you're this upset."

"I can drive!" He yelled, tears sequinning his eyelashes.

"You shouldn't. You could have an accident."

"YOU...Y—" He howled like an animal hollowed from retching. Mohammed's tears cut loose, and his head fell on my shoulder.

Really breaking teacher-student protocol, I folded my arm around him and patted his back, careful not to onramp a road to flirtation. "Go find Diyako and be with your friend, but please don't drive." I looked over his posse, of which Zoran seemed the most stoic. "Zoran, can you drive?" In 2017, Kurds couldn't apply for a driving license until they were 18 years old, and not every eighteen-year-old had one.

Zoran nodded.

I dropped my hand from Mohammed's back. "Mohammed, give Zoran your car keys." I hoped my telling-not-asking voice transferred outside the classroom.

When Zoran opened the driver-side door, I ran back to the classroom. About half the students had left, the other half sitting and talking in Kurdish or Arabic. I quickly checked my email to see if a directive had come down from admin. We were to finish out the morning session, but essentially, the teaching day was skunked. When I invited the remaining students to sit in a circle and talk about their feelings, they gathered like recalcitrant family members, psychologically chained to a dinner table. They spoke a few words between longer and longer pauses. We all kept an eye on the clock mounted near the door, its white face suspended in the gloom like a lantern, marking the way home.

The Go Bag

We stood in a circle on the sidewalk at the back of our apartment building, passing a bottle, roguing fear with tequila. The December dusk time air was grey, the color of waiting. The ground shook again, and the tower blocks near our own swayed like hula dancers.

When the first tremors started, I had been writing in my bedroom, vaguely registering the man-sized armoire doors rattling to my left. My roommate, JJ, pinballed down the hallway leading from the living room to my room, yelling we had to leave *now* before he cannonballed out. Breaking my gaze from the keyboard, I took in the seemingly rippling furniture and grabbed my laptop, cursing myself for not having a go bag prepped, especially given the last few months. A go bag is a pre-packed bag stocked with the essentials: cash, debit and credit cards, computers, passports, phones, chargers, and medications if you take any, ready to grab on the fly for immediate evacuation. I had never considered a go bag until after 9/11, when my dad suggested I prep one and know my escape routes if New York City were attacked again. When he advised me to pack cigarettes because they could be traded for currency (He was a child in Berlin during World War II.), a flare-up of teenage disdain dismissed the thought of a go bag from my mind entirely.

JJ shouted from the living room, "Hurry up. The TV is wobbling." And then, "I'm taking your tequila bottle, okay?" before hustling out of our seventh-floor apartment door, his go bag balanced smugly on his shoulder. In the stairwell, we met up with Mark and Sofia, a married couple who were always disaster ready.

Two sets of computer bags filled with laptops, backup storage devices, thumbnail drives, paper copies of important documents, and ziplocked bags of nuts freighted their arms. Instead of running out the front of the building as we had during November's 7.3 magnitude earthquake a month earlier, we headed out the back door, away from the faculty coiling like cigarette smoke down the stairwell and out of the building. As I was bringing up the rear, I simply followed the tequila.

"This quake isn't as strong as the last one," JJ said before swigging from the bottle and then passing it to Sofia.

The last one was the first one most of us had experienced at the university, so there hadn't been an earthquake protocol in place. There still wasn't. During the first one, again, I had been working in my room, and again, JJ had to come tell me to get out. That time, I hadn't even grabbed my computer before we scurried to the front parking lot with the rest of the faculty and waited like overly-mothered children for someone to tell us what to do. That time, I didn't panic as we watched to see if our building would fall down. I panicked after. Discovering a fresh labyrinth of cracks in our living room wall or the lattice of frown lines scoring the elevator shaft in the hallway made my heart dance at the speed of machine gun fire. Luckily, our city had been spared the misfortune of geography. Closer to the epicenter near the Iran-Iraq border, hundreds of people had been killed, and thousands more had been injured in the decomposing streets whereas our city had suffered only a handful of casualties.

Sofia drank and then checked her phone. "5.4. The epicenter is near Halabja." Her frozen breath haloed her face.

Halabja, a city made famous by toxoid apple gas and Saddam Hussein's genocidal ambitions, was about 40 miles away. I held out my hand for the bottle. "This sort of reminds me of the second fire." I gulped the counterfeit Patron silver, and a pebble of tequila dribbled off my chin.

"Been there, done that?" Mark shivered a bit in the December chill. None of us had grabbed warm coats.

"Second fire?" JJ tried to underreact.

The tequila sparked loose in my chest like a blown dandelion puff as I handed Mark the bottle.

"Before your time, JJ. Before your time." Mark had been employed by the university for the longest, catching the tail end of the John Agresto days, when hundred-dollar bills helicoptered the campus like laughing confetti. Before John Agresto was the academic dean and chancellor of our university, he had served as the education advisor for the Coalition Provisional Authority, which ran the US occupation under Paul Bremer. "The fire in Asher's apartment was the second."

The second fire was legendary among the faculty, and not just because it had damaged most of the apartments on the ninth floor. Asher, the grandson of a foreign diplomat and a possible future founder of a men's rights group, embroidered the facts on how the fire had started. In one version, a spark from the wall-mounted electric split herkied onto the sofa, igniting it. Another version not built to last featured an electrical surge in the wiring, which magicked a fire in his flat screen TV. A final origin story whispered of an unattended space heater pushed too close to an easy chair. When responsibility for the fire pointed in Asher's direction, he allegedly engaged his students to research a defense. Later, Asher accused the university's maintenance workers of stealing his wife's jewelry after they moved his family's belonging into an undamaged apartment so the university could repair the scorched one. Yet, inexplicably, Asher remained employed. Hearing these stories, I could picture a young Asher in a boarding school uniform, holding a clarinet.

"There was another fire, JJ. The year before, almost to the day." I remembered because that fire had happened on my birthday. Jeni, a colleague who liked to quip indignantly, "How do you sleep with yourself?" when you'd admit to doing something stupid or humiliating, and I had just returned from an afternoon booze at the Lalazar Hotel, which catered to foreigners and the Kurdish elite alike. We had drunk latinos, a concoction I hadn't known until moving to Sulaimaniyah. This elixir boasted one shot of tequila sunk, shot glass and all, into a lager and topped off with fresh lemon juice, the glass rim garlanded in salt and sumac.

Two latinos was my usual, self-imposed limit. When Jeni and I approached our apartment building and saw a shrieking figure trapped by a silent cloud of smoke on a tenth-floor balcony, we hauled ass up the stairs to knock on doors as our friends and colleagues streamed out in untidy waves. We'd drunk three latinos a piece, which revisited my mouth just to remind me they were there, as we climbed with bleating speed from floor to floor all the way to the top, our stomached lined with unhelpful Fattoush salad.

"Wasn't Estrella in her bathrobe?" Mark smirked.

At the time of the first fire, Estrella, the deeply unliked interim president of the university, lived on the top floor of our building. Not having a fire protocol in place either, we scurried like field mice out of the building and skidded to a stop in the front parking lot, uncertainty hounding our backs. Milling around in sweatpants or blue jeans under our jackets, we watched orange-yellow flames lick living rooms through shivering windows and waited for someone to take charge. Estrella kept her arms folded across the triangle of bony flesh visible beneath her fuzzy robe and said nothing.

The fire burned robustly, drawing a crowd of spectators from the other apartment blocks in our compound. Azade, one of my adult English students in the professional development institute, came rushing over to see if I was okay. She invited me to stay in her sister's apartment in the compound. Word of the fire traveled fast because after I spoke with Azade, Ziryan, one of her classmates, sped over in his SUV to see if I needed anything. Their unconditional kindness was a mantle around my shoulders.

"Remember the hotel they evacuated us to?" Sofia took the bottle from Mark, a conspiratorial glint to her eye.

Mark emitted a xylophone tinkle of laughter. "I remember the armed guard escort to it."

The armed guard escort did feel excessive.

Once the fire was out, we were allowed back inside by floor number and given five minutes to pack overnight bags before the university shuttle took us to a local hotel. Fearing another blaze might ignite, I stuffed my computer, passport, a roll of hundreds[1], antique jewelry, childhood bird puppets, one-of-a-kind dresses, and teaching materials into a suitcase, which I clunked onto the bus. Bumping it down the narrow aisle, I met a hint of infant wonder from the drowsing sleepers already seated, small backpacks nestled between their feet. Since most of the faculty and staff living in our building were Westerners, a convoy of Peshmerga soldiers perched in an open-bed truck with their Kalashnikovs drawn, accompanied us out of the compound and down the moon-blued road, four whole blocks to a hotel.

"You're kidding?" JJ reached for the bottle, already sliding on the scale from one to shitload.

"Nope." I also remembered the party my next-door neighbor Luke organized in someone's hotel room. One minute Jeni and I were unpacking in a shared room whose bathroom was a cry for help.

---

1 Back then, we were paid in cash because a fiscal crisis had caused the government to freeze some banks' current accounts. After payday, we'd go to a local NGO which needed dollars for operating expenses on the ground in Iraq, Kurdistan, and Syria. The NGO would take our cash and transfer an equal amount into our Stateside bank accounts from its Stateside bank account, and we'd avoid an annoying errand and pricey transfer fees.)

In the next, Luke was herding us to another room draped in velvet curtains ripe with stale cigarette smoke. As I had never met some of the other faculty before, the impromptu gathering reminded me of a Christmas party at an insurance office, but the intimate gesture of sharing a bottle removed the space between us. Counterfeit bourbon distilled in a moment of revenge soaked up my thoughts before it drained straight into the pain nook of my brain.

JJ passed Sofia the tequila, which took another turn around the four of us before it expired.

"Do you think we can go back in?" I knew that asking was like asking how long string is. But still.

"What's the rush?" JJ eyed the surrounding buildings. Behind them, the mountains wore a toupee of old snow.

"I'm hungry and I have to grade." Nearing the end of the term, I had a pile of essays to read. Their overall coherence was as likely as the freshness of gas station sweet rolls. I would need a detonation of time to work through them.

Mark peered thought the back door windows. "I think I see people entering the front."

The night sounds, shouty children and rumbling buildings creaking, "Fuck me, fuck you," quieted.

JJ's fingers closed around the doorknob like a tulip going to sleep.

"We'd better take the stairs," Sofia resettled the bags shagging her shoulders.

Panic lapsed into numb history. The term had tossed with tumult, and I was tired. I pitched the tequila bottle into the trash before ambling back inside, my feet rising and falling on the stairs, bicycling slowly home.

Seven

Baghdad, Iraq 2018

Wasta

"You'll need to keep a low profile," Rif said, concerned for my safety.

I was grinning from ear to ear, head bobbing like a car dashboard dog ornament. "Yes!" and then, "Thank you."

I was going to Baghdad!

It was spring, 2018, and a Baghdad visa, difficult to obtain before President Masoud Barzani's push for Kurdish independence, was now nearly impossible. Barzani's ill-fated 2017 independence referendum had resulted in military conflict between the Kurdish government and the Iraqi government, and Iraq had won. Kurdistan lost territory, including the oil-rich fields of Kirkuk, and the ability to control its borders. Now, the only flights operating out of Kurdish airports led to cities in the Iraqi-controlled south, where visas were required to transfer onto international flights.

The sole reason I had the visa was *wasta*, the power of connections to get what you want. The chicken to *wasta*'s egg is access. The private university in Kurdistan for which I worked was founded by the then president of Iraq, and the university had used his *wasta* to obtain travel visas for its foreign faculty so that they could go home for Christmas a few months prior. Without the visas, it would have been impossible for anyone to leave the Kurdish region regardless of their passport. The university was one of the only institutions in our city to secure visas for its foreign nationals. The makeshift visa system was so new that the director of my program was the first American to travel from Kurdistan through Baghdad to the

United States while the Kurdish borders were closed, and the visa processing system in the Baghdad International Airport had not been fully set up.

(I would lose my Baghdad visa a few months later when I was robbed in Spain. The next time I had to go to Baghdad to train teachers for the Ministry of Higher Education, our head of security, a man of great *wasta* because his brother had taken a bullet for the current president of Iraq, walked me through passport control and into Iraq without a visa. Someone handwrote a visa equivalent into my passport in ballpoint pen, and I used that to enter Iraq alone in 2019 on a recruitment mission for the university.)

I hated that I wasn't brave enough to put my fresh visa to good use and explore Baghdad on my own. Even though I had lived in New York City for twelve years, Baghdad intimidated me the way Mars might; alien and aweing and possibly dangerous. I have a negative sense of direction, and Baghdad is colossal. It stretches north and south along both banks of the Tigris River as it sprawls east and west onto the surrounding plains for a mighty total of 260 square miles. I knew I would get hopelessly lost, and my Arabic vocabulary consisted of seven words. Also, as a solo foreign female, I wasn't sure if I'd be safe on the streets. I had suffered street harassment many times in Kurdistan, the reputationally liberal-minded, secular north. I wasn't sure what would happen in the traditionally more conservative, religious south. Despite the liberation of Mosul, ISIS was still sporadically detonating bombs in Baghdad. Anything could happen.

Ambition knows no contradictions. I heard that Rif had taken some of my colleagues around Baghdad, so I asked if I could tag along the next time he went there. Rif surprised me by saying he going to present a paper at an international language arts and translations conference in a few weeks, and he could check if there was an opportunity for me to present something too. I am not an academic, nor do I hold a PHD. This might be the time to confess that Rif had liked me romantically two years prior. When I decided that I didn't want to pursue a romantic liaison, we morphed into an awkward friendship because Rif's seriousness drew out my juvenile side, which is an acquired taste. I hoped he hadn't misinterpreted my Baghdad inquiry as an invitation to induce religious outbursts between bedsheets if we attended the conference together.

Raised by an immigrant father and a traditional homemaker mother in the 1970s, I wasn't taught how to show up for myself and ask for what I wanted. My learning curve was a pendulum swinging between timid hints and privileged-fuel demands until I got "the ask" right. My trip to Baghdad was the result of getting the ask right. Thanks to Rif's *wasta*, I was going to run a workshop on student-centered teaching at the conference, which was being held at one of the oldest institutions of higher learning in the world. I was thrilled to be on my way to Baghdad, a palimpsest of dynasties, caliphs, and occupiers, treading in that liminal space between dulled grandeur and war.

Rif felt responsible for my security, partly because he had facilitated my Baghdad opportunity and partly because, a long time ago, he had to run for his life in Baghdad. As a conscripted Iraqi who spoke English in Saddam's army during the 1993 invasion, he was tasked with eavesdropping on the US forces' military communications to determine their locations so Saddam's army could bomb them. Time after time, Rif misreported the coordinates to his superiors to spare lives. Alone at his post one night, he received an anonymous phone call telling him "they" were coming for him. Run, Rif. Run!, which he did, smuggling himself north through the Kurdish region and across dubious borders where he encountered a US military convoy and pled for asylum.

Through someone's *wasta*, we were met at the Baghdad International Airport by two men, a driver and a representative of Prime Minister Haider al-Abadi's government. We were taken through the Green Zone, once the government center for the Coalition Provisional Authority during the US occupation of Iraq. Now, the British, American, Australian, and Egyptian embassies, as well as some private military contractors, called the Green Zone home. Our escorts insisted on stopping in front of the July 14th Statue, a monument of three soldiers set high atop a marble base, commemorating the army's overthrow of the monarchy in 1958, to take pictures with me. Was it because I was an American woman or an honored guest? I had found that in Middle Eastern patriarchal societies, being a Western woman put me in a class of my own; not as high in status as a man, but higher than that of a local woman. At that moment, being American was my only currency as a woman. Unfortunately, I lacked the agency to spend it because declining the photo request would have insulted our high-ranking hosts. I was caught in a web of *wasta*.

We were dropped at a hotel in the Karrada district, where less than two years prior, a car bomb had ripped through a major shopping street killing 125 people and injuring 150 more. ISIS had claimed responsibility for that attack and for a very recent bombing in al-Tayaran Square, which had killed thirty-five people. All eyes were on me as we crossed the hotel lobby's cream tiled floor. I was the only American woman in the lobby, possibly the building. Some people stared because they were unaccustomed to seeing unguarded, non-Kevlar-vested Western women in their war-torn city. Others stared because they assumed all foreign women in hotels were prostitutes. My *wasta* had turned to kryptonite.

It is hard to take in your surroundings while keeping your head down. It reminded me of having to shower in freezing cold water and trying not to get wet. As I was waiting to check in, I glanced around the lobby while purposefully not looking directly at anyone. The molten brown leather couches reminded me of stacked Ho Ho chocolate snack cakes. Interspersed between the couches were sets of electric tomato-red tapestry chairs. I nudged Rif, who was in front of me in line. "Those chairs would make an awesome coat."

Rif turned to stare at me like a man aghast with realization.

"They would! There's a designer in New York who makes coats out of tapestries."

Rif answered with his back.

I leaned forward, speaking over his shoulder. "Thanks again for bringing me to Baghdad."

*

The next morning, I found Rif sitting in one of the tomato chairs grading exams as he and other conference presenters waited for our drivers to take us to the conference site. He was less friendly than he had been the night before. Our evening had started out by visiting Karrada's sights: the Kahramana Fountain, which depicts a scene from *Ali Baba and the Forty Thieves* but had come to symbolize the US occupation after the 2003 invasion; the National Theatre, dark behind its reinforced blast walls, and a big shop selling all types of musical instruments. Away from the hotel, Rif cautioned me not to speak English on the streets, presumably for my safety. We stopped at a liquor store, where he had me wait outside while he gathered some provisions (Life lesson: never travel without a wine opener, especially in countries where drinking alcohol is *haram*.), and then we returned to the hotel. After a few drinks, I called it a night to seek the comforts of solitude alone in my room.

My eyes ping-ponged between Rif's chair and an empty couch adjacent to it before I finally sat down. "Morning."

The crown of his Rif's bobbed slightly.

I was reaching inside my handbag for my workshop notes when an older gentleman joined me on the sofa. Clocking his mustache, grey hair, and polyblend suit, I figured him to be another professor attending the conference although he looked like a day player from *Law & Order: Special Victims Unit.* He'd be the kind of character who owned a convenience store with a shady side hustle run out of the back. I felt this stranger hovering at the edge of conversation, waiting for an opening, while I tried to make small talk with Rif so that this stranger would turn away. When Rif answered dismissively, the stranger pressed his advantage with a compliment to my blue dress.

Listen closely to the stories people tell you, and you might hear their ambitions underneath. The older gentleman couldn't wait to let me know that he was speaking at a conference that day. In fact, he had been asked to give the introductory welcome speech! I didn't have the heart to tell him that I had been asked to give that same speech four days prior and had declined because of the short notice. Then, he told me about his job, his children, and his wife, in that order, before he asked me the usual demographic questions, including my age. When I told him that I was fifty-one, he was shocked because he was only a few years older than I, but we looked very different. He remarked that I must have had an easy life. After I told him not to make assumptions about the ease of my life, my American privilege backhanded me across the face and then finger-flicked my forehead for good measure. Who was I to argue with a man who had grown up in a war-torn country about the ease of life? Chagrined, I told him that I taught at a university in Sulaimaniyah, to which he remarked that he lived about an hour away and would like to see me again. I declined, mad at myself for letting my guard down.

Someone called into the lobby in Arabic, and Rif, who had said nothing during this exchange, told me it was time to leave as he started packing up his things. Only when the three of us headed for the same van did the aspirational adulterer realize I was attending the same conference as he. I wondered what he thought I had been doing, loitering in the hotel lobby, when in reality, I had been doing the same as he: looking for a ride, just not in the biblical sense.

The Second Wife

The conference was hosted by a Shiite university in Baghdad, where seventy people had been killed and over 139 had been wounded in a triple bomb attack conducted by Sunni insurgents in 2007. We vended through an assembly line of security checks and popped out onto a crowded, sandstone campus. The courtyard swarmed with students, academics, university staff, security, and cameras. Just as Rif reminded me to keep a low profile, Dr. Obedi, the woman who had facilitated my attending the conference and asked that I give the welcome speech, approached us. She asked if I would agree to be interviewed for a local television station.

I looked to Rif, who should have been the person being interviewed, but he wanted no part of it. Because I felt bad about declining her request to give the welcome speech and because I like the limelight, I said yes. In reality, I had been asked to give a short interview on the grounds of a prominent Shiite university, on an Arabic TV station, speaking in English to an Arabic interviewer with minimal English language skills, for an Arabic audience because I am an American woman, and for that reason only. Although the US and the predominantly Shiite Popular Mobilization Forces (PMF) had worked together to defeat ISIS, the endemic discord between the US and Iran, and the political fallout between the US and former Prime Minister Nuri Al-Maliki's Shiite-dominated government powered suspicion and distrust between the Shiites and the US. In this context, the visual of my being interviewed on Arabic TV was geopolitical eye candy.

I wasn't giving my workshop until the second day of the conference, so Dr. Obedi showed me around the campus while Rif attended some of the presentations being held in Arabic. I was fascinated by this elegant, petite, well-educated, and well-spoken Arabic woman. She seemed so modern compared to what I had expected her to be. I was dying to know her point of view on gender-based issues, so I broached the subject by asking what she thought about the upcoming elections. Legally, twenty-five percent of parliamentary seats had to be filled by women as outlined in the 2004 interim constitution created by the Iraqi Governing Council. I had seen several posters and billboards advertising female parliamentary candidates, smiling broadly in their hijabs, on the drive from the Green Zone to the hotel.

"I don't support equal rights," Dr. Obedi tossed the statement over her shoulder as I followed her through the campus grounds.

My jaw dropped. Dr. Obedi, dressed in a long white skirt, vertical black and white striped top, and black cardigan, her hair anchored by sunglasses and flowing past her shoulders, held a prominent position at the university. "But you have a career."

"Yes, I do."

"May I ask you a personal question?" I waited for Dr. Obedi to nod. "Are you married?"

"I'm not. I live with my parents and one sister, who is also unmarried."

I guessed Dr. Obedi to be in her early forties. "May I ask why you don't support equal rights?"

"I don't need to. My family allowed me to be educated, to have a career. I have everything that I want without the government saying I should have it."

"What about the women whose families are not open-minded and won't allow them to be educated? How can they have a life like yours if there isn't gender equality legislation?"

As we reached Dr. Obedi's office, she removed her sunglasses, setting her hair free. A small smile played across her lips. "A government mandate won't help those women. None of those women in Parliament have any real power. They are there to fill a quota."

"Isn't that all the more reason to push for equal rights legislation, so women can attain real power and move society forward?"

Dr. Obedi looked at me as though she expected nothing less from an American woman.

I had encountered a similar judgment, a cocktail of "naïve child" mixed with a pinch of scorn, when I had taught in Kyiv. My Ukrainian students, who were mostly gorgeous, twenty-something women with perfectly done makeup and bottle blond hair, told me that American women were dumb, for what was wrong with a man paying for your dinner, lighting your cigarette, holding a door open for you, or leaving some pocket money on the dresser when he left your bed in the morning? At the time, my own Ukrainian boyfriend had offered to pay my salary so I wouldn't take a summer position at a sister school in another city. When I pointed out that he had just offered to pay for my company and how my culture understood that transaction, he reddened and apologized, because in his culture, paying your girlfriend to stick around was not viewed as prostitution. Neither the Muslim women nor the Slavic women I had taught considered American women to be feminine, with their outspoken manner, confident stride, and constant cry for equality.

"Not all progress benefits society." Dr. Obedi said from behind her desk as she gestured for me to sit.

I didn't press her to explain. Over the years I had been in northern Iraq, I had heard many people, including Kurds, despite Saddam's genocidal Anfal campaign, Assyrians, and Arabs, say life was better under Saddam than it was after the US invasion to "liberate the Iraqi people" and "spread democracy across the Arab world."

Dr. Obedi's office had sofas flanking the walls on either side of her desk. I took a seat near her so I could watch this intriguing woman, whose gracious exterior belied her steely resolve. Her female faculty trickled in, not so much to meet me, but to see her. You could sense how well the faculty liked one another and respected Dr. Obedi by the candor of their conversation.

The day's gossip was about a top administrator's choice of a second wife. The faculty discussing this choice included a flirtatious poet who looked like a young Penelope Cruz; a gutsy, middle-aged, blue-eyed translations expert who wore her headscarf tied like a turban to show the front of her light hair; and an erudite academic in a black hijab and chador, who held two PHDs and was researching homosexuality in the Ottoman Empire just months after ISIS had thrown homosexuals off the tops of buildings. Having never been privy to Kurdish women's intimate conversations, I was ecstatic to be included in this one. I marveled at the Iraqi women's frankness in front of me, a total stranger, after about ten minutes of pleasantries. Later, an American friend who has worked in Iraq for over fifteen years explained that because I did not know these women's relatives and therefore could not report what they'd shared, they probably felt comfortable to speak freely in front of me.

The women didn't have a problem with the existence of the second wife per se, but they were perplexed by the top administrator's choice because the second wife was neither markedly younger nor prettier. According to the translations expert, the only discernible difference was that the top administrator could have sex with his old wife in Arabic and his new wife in English because the new wife spoke it fluently. Working in linguistics, the other women found this very funny.

I was reminded of a man I had once met in an Erbil nightclub, a place filled with the contradictory air of Middle Eastern culture and Western decadence. There was the sweet, powdery scent of fruity shisha smoke and the polyrhythmic percussion of traditional Kurdish music juxtaposed with cocooning leather banquettes and a fully-stocked bar. The man was a rumored hitman for one of the ruling political families of Kurdistan. He looked like an extra from *The Sopranos*, with a stout build cloaked in a black, double-breasted suit and a face you'd see on a post office flier. Each inside pocket of his suit jacket packed a pistol, which, despite the security screening and mandatory gun check at the nightclub's entrance, he wore into the nightclub. Getting his guns through the security check meant he had *wasta*.

He joined our table, which included a hedonist who was also an advisor on religious affairs to the Kurdish government, the hedonist's male cousin, and me. Between rounds of tequila shots and puffs of watermelon and mint-flavored shisha tobacco from a hookah pipe, the rumored hitman, who was also attending law school part time, complained to us about his foreign-born wife who looked "exactly like Angelina Jolie" and whom he was "tired of fucking." If she really did look like Angelina Jolie, being young and pretty had nothing to do with his desire to have sex with someone different. Our genetic wiring to crave novelty in sex was at play, but that wiring crackles in both men and women.

I listened to the women in Dr. Obedi's office condone the taking of second wives with forensic attention. Because I hate being second-best or feeling left out, I couldn't fathom accepting a cultural practice which provoked either.

A held tongue chafes.

I spit out my thought. "Men shouldn't be allowed to take a second wife unless women are allowed to take a second husband."

All the women looked at me as though I were mentally malfunctioning.

"It's only fair that if men get to do something, women should get to do it, too," I added, trying to dislodge my foot from my mouth.

Dr. Obedi piped up from behind her desk. "Alex is a feminist."

The other women exchanged looks before focusing their attention back on me. The translations expert was the first to speak. "You are thinking like a man."

"How so?"

"Men need sex. It is a need. It is different for women."

"Women need sex as much as men do."

The translations expert shook her head. "Men *need* sex. Every day, every day, every day. They don't care if they put it there or there or there," she pointed to all sides of the room.

"So do women." I wondered about her own marriage. "What about the emotional fulfilment you receive from your partner?"

"Now, you are thinking like a woman. Men are not emotional with sex. They need it, need it, need it." The translations expert slapped the back of her hand into the palm of the other every time she said need. "They don't care where."

"What about individual temperament? Some men are emotional about sex. Some women need a lot of sex."

The academic in black spoke up. "My husband threatens to take a second wife, and I tell him to go ahead. Please. Do it. I dare you. But he never does."

My American privilege clamped its hand over my mouth. Iraq's Personal Status Law stipulates Iraqi constitutional rulings on marriage, divorce, alimony, wills, inheritance and family, affording some legal protections for women. I wondered if such protections were theoretical because a person wishing to divorce a spouse must file a suit in a Sharia court. Since the fall of Saddam, there had been a growing movement to abolish the Personal Status Law and implement the laws of Islamic Sharia. Constitutional amendments such as the Ja-afari Law, which limits women's rights and facilitates polygamy for men, had been proposed. If the academic in black divorced her husband, she might lose her children, her status in society, her home, and possibly her wealth. Urging her husband to take a second wife was a coping mechanism for being bullied in her unhappy marriage.

"Maybe the big boss took a second wife to get that rush that comes from a new attraction," I said. "Maybe he's trying to feel alive."

"Now, you sound like an American. After years of war, we know what it is to feel alive." The translations expert said this kindly.

My American privilege slid its bony fingers around my neck and squeezed. My face red-hotted.

The translations expert waved my embarrassment away. "Anyway, you should see him with his first wife. I bet they have sex like monkeys."

You Call Yourself a Feminist

Dr. Obedi asked if I would mind meeting some students. Two skinny eighteen-or-nineteen-year-old boys, eager to meet an American, pushed each other into Dr. Obedi's office. The first thing they did was thank me for coming to their campus, which surprised me. A few weeks prior, an undergraduate lecturer from the university where the conference was being held had observed my class in Sulaimaniyah as part of a teacher training program organized by Iraq's Ministry of Higher Education. When I asked him what most Iraqis in Baghdad thought about Americans, he told me they blamed Americans for the ruin of their country. Yet, here were two teens, giggly and excited to practice their English with a native speaker. They told me they had never met an American before and hoped to come to the United States because they loved Hollywood movies. No female students came to see me in Dr. Obedi's office.

Other male university faculty came in and out of Dr. Obedi's office to meet the American woman visiting the campus, including a large imposing man with a huge, jewel-encrusted ring on his right hand and an ungifted face. Earlier, I had noticed several of the academics and security personnel on the campus quad, sporting similar rings. Rif later told me that these rings symbolize being a Shiite Muslim and paid homage to Imam Ali, the first Caliph and Imam after the prophet Muhammad.

Ring Man walked right up to me, stopping inches from my face before he demanded to take a photo together. There was no room for me to back up because a sofa was directly behind me, so

I tried to count his eyebrow hairs. If I had been in my own office, I would have told him to get out of my face, but I did not want to reflect poorly on Dr. Obedi or Rif. I stole a look at Dr. Obedi, who was in the middle of a phone call. To my horror, Ring Man demanded Dr. Obedi come "at once" and take a photo of us. Here he was, in her office, ordering her to interrupt what she was doing to serve him even though I was pretty sure that she outranked him. Dr. Obedi turned slightly away from us, speaking into the phone as her hand covered her mouth and the mouthpiece. I had a strong urge to protect her.

Ring Man turned back to me. "You going to read my master's thesis."

Say what? Glancing at Dr. Obedi, I wondered how rude I could be to this giant man-baby. To be fair, Ring Man had about an intermediate level of fluency, and sometimes non-native speakers use incorrect syntax, which results in their questions sounding like statements, but Ring Man's tone lacked upwards inflection. He bellowed demands. Based on his spoken English, I could imagine how poorly his thesis had been written, and the thought of reviewing it made my hair hurt.

"You will to give the notes. Improving the English."

Suspicion confirmed.

Ring Man hollered again at Dr. Obedi, who was hanging up the phone. To my surprise, she immediately rounded her desk and politely asked for his mobile. As soon as the photo was taken, he snatched up his phone, told me again that I would read his thesis, and exited.

"How important is he?" I asked Dr. Obedi.

"Not very. Why?"

"I can't believe the way he spoke to you."

Dr. Obedi gave a small laugh. "That was nothing."

I wasn't sure I believed her. "I don't like when anyone, especially men, speak to me that way."

"I don't like it either."

"Then, why were you so nice to him?"

"Why not be nice?"

"Because he was disrespectful."

"And he will be again. I cannot change him, so I smile and let him think he has power over me. But I will remember this, and when I am ready, I will use it."

What a badass! I admired her self-control. "So then, I don't have to read his thesis?"

It was Dr. Obedi's turn to look dubious.

"I'll read it if not reading it makes you look bad."

"And you call yourself a feminist," she teased.

*

Dr. Obedi and I attended a few conference sessions while we waited for the other women to finish teaching. As we passed a presentation hall, she offhandedly remarked that the Shiite militia had "buried the bodies under there." Although Shiite forces guarded the campus, I got the feeling that most of the female faculty I had met resented their presence. The translations expert told me the Shiite forces guarding the campus threatened some female faculty and staff whom the Shiite thought should cover their heads, which was why the translations expert started wearing her head scarf after her husband died a few years earlier. Her sliding it back to expose the front of her hair was her act of defiance. There was another widow among us, a grey-skinned, melancholic professor who still wore mourning clothes although her husband had been disappeared four years prior. When she showed me photos of her and husband taken shortly before he was disappeared, I almost gasped at her vibrancy radiating from the photo. I glanced up at the melancholy professor. Grief had literally drained her of color and vitality. The sex pest from the hotel sofa was right; I had had an easy life.

Dr. Obedi, the Penelope Cruz lookalike poet, the academic in black, the melancholy academic, and I loaded ourselves into a taxi for a trip to Mutanabbi Street, the historic booksellers' street and Shahbandar café, where intellectuals, poets, and politicians have gathered inside its framed-photo lined walls to drink Baghdadi lemon tea and debate for the past one hundred years. We would finish our daytrip at the Tigris River, along which Iraqis were again enjoying masgouf, a dish of grilled carp seasoned with olive oil, rock salt, tamarind, and ground turmeric. Before we left the campus grounds, Dr. Obedi cautioned me not to speak English in the car, and the Penelope Cruz poet suggested everyone call me Leila to draw less attention to my Western-ness.

The taxi was narrow, so three of us squeezed into the hot back seat, leaving the Penelope Cruz poet and the academic in black to sit up front. As the youngest, the Penelope Cruz poet immediately surrendered the passenger seat to the academic in black before wedging herself half on the academic in black's lap and half on the center console. Our taxi driver, an old man with eyebrows of ancient relief and a formidable nose drooping over a bushy white mustache, wasn't sure he wanted two passengers sharing one front seat, but the Penelope Cruz poet, alternating between feisty and beguiling, prevailed. As the taxi driver took one of Baghdad's many roundabouts like a race car driver, he turned to her, raising his voice as he raised his hand from the steering wheel. I held my breath, half expecting him to backhand her. Turning coquettish, she said something in Arabic and punctuated it with an impish grin. The taxi driver's irritation dissolved amid his laughter and ours.

As we wandered among the book stalls lining Mutanabbi Street towards the Tigris, I thought about how my new acquaintances navigated through patriarchy instead of assaulting it head-on as I did, which often resulted in my getting "the ask" wrong. Perhaps there were other ways. I recalled an Elizabeth Dole interview in which she observed that American feminists attack to get what they want whereas traditional American women charm. The Penelope Cruz look alike poet also wielded charm. Hers was a heady mixture of seduction, impetuousness, and humor, which could rival Sophia Loren's. The translations expert claimed little victories in the tilt of a turban. Dr. Obedi went along to get along, patiently waiting for her moment to strike. The academic in black turned her husband's threats into dares to defy a bully and retain her agency. Instead of dismantling patriarchy, these women worried its cracks, creating tiny pockets of space for themselves, much like how rainwater, churning carbonic acid, slowly hollows rock to form caves.

Eight

Sulaimaniayh, Kurdistan, Iraq 2019

Don't Say a Word

"Al, I think I fucked up," Luke announced.

I stopped typing. Seeing Luke was agitated, I shut my computer. Usually, nothing much fazed him. When our apartment block caught on fire, and we were evacuated to a questionable hotel, and when our apartment block was rocked to and fro by a 7.3 Richter scale earthquake, Luke's reaction was to organize a party. He made luxury out of a moment.

"What happened?" I asked, unsure I wanted to know. Even though Luke often referred to me as a sister, we were very different. I was a disciplined, by-the-book, future-dweller whereas Luke lived his life as if it were the last tube of toothpaste. He squeezed every possible bit of joy and pleasure from it, rules be damned. Years ago, we had been dancing at a club on a UN compound, pretentious with its door policy that favored females. Luke, wearing a fedora, his shirt unbuttoned past decency into display, moved like he was born from music. He was trying to teach me how to move my hips, saying I didn't know how to let go. By the time I traded the dance floor for a bar stool, he had gotten three phone numbers. After hooking up with an NGO worker, he came home, escorted by sunrise as birds tweeted jazz.

Luke paced back and forth across the hand-me-down Persian carpet covering my living room floor. Through the windows behind him, the Iraqi sun sizzled the phallic blue skyscraper towering above Sulaimaniyah's stunted cityscape. He was days away from leaving the Kurdish region for good. I was sad to see him go, but everything fresh has a shelf life. He was no longer the committed teacher I had met eight years prior on the plane to Erbil, where we both had teaching jobs at an elite international school. Now, we both worked for a prestigious private university in Erbil's rival city of Sulaimaniyah. The year prior, he had devised a scheme to dismiss his university prep classes an hour or so early several times a week for most of the term, cheating his students out of countless instruction hours until he got caught. Luke knew it was time for him to move on. He had zeroed out his student loans, made bank, and was burnt crisp by teaching. His plans to start a marijuana farm on a friend's plot of California acreage had fallen through, so now he was pressed for Plan B.

Luke stopped pacing. "You know how I went to that woman's house last night?"

A few nights before, I had taken Luke out for a farewell dinner at a hotel which catered to foreigners. After, we stopped at a local lounge on the way back to our apartment block, where we were next door neighbors. I left as Luke, his Asian cheeks flushed a telltale alcoholic red, bummed a cigarette from a dark-haired woman sitting alone at the bar. I assumed he would hit on her and didn't want to be a third wheel. It turned out the woman was married, and she had invited Luke over to her house to do drugs with her and her husband a few days later. Because Kurdistan has a zero-tolerance drug policy, I thought Luke should steer clear, but I kept my thoughts to myself. It wasn't my place to tell him how to live.

"Man, that woman was wearing her pajama bottoms at the bar," Luke said in the same tone he used when he'd poke my belly and tell me to suck it in.

"I thought they were yoga pants." I hadn't really looked at her because I was a practiced wingman. Back in Erbil, I had run interference for Luke when he dated a friend of mine under our supervisor's nose. Our supervisor happened to be his ex, and the supervisor, Luke, and I lived on the same floor in the same wing on a different compound in a different city a different life ago. Those were the before days: before the Syrian refugee crisis and ISIS and economic collapse had brought Kurdistan to its knees. It was 2019, and the world's attention had moved on from Iraq.

"And she and her husband are loaded. Like, when I went to their house, I dressed UP."

I pictured Luke in his cornflower blue dress shirt with the white collar and his aviators hanging in the V of his black four-button vest. "So, how'd you fuck up?"

Luke finally sat down on my sofa, which was the twin of the one in his apartment. "I think the husband might have taken photos of me." His lips duckbilled as his eyebrows raised. "Cutting lines of coke."

I kept my face very still even though I had little patience for Luke's destructive behavior. I knew he was anxious about moving back to the States, about setting up a new life in an old place that didn't quite fit anymore, so I kept my finger off his sore. I neither condoned his drug use nor berated him for it because our friendship had been built on a "You do you" policy. As a result, we didn't hang out together much. I was a repository for Luke's secrets while he encouraged me to loosen up and live a little. "What do you mean 'think'? Do you know for certain?"

"No."

"Then maybe he didn't."

"The husband was asking a lot of questions, like where I work and when I leave."

"He could have just been making conversation."

"Or he could want to blackmail me, and Al… Al, I let my guard down."

"No ones going to blackmail you." I laughed at the ridiculousness of it. "Let's say he was. When do you leave?"

"Next Tuesday or Wednesday. After Eid."

"You don't even know, so how can he?"

"Yeah, you're probably right." Luke relaxed into the sofa.

"What did you cut the lines with?"

"My faculty ID and my residency card."

I shook my head. "If the edges of the cards are frayed, there might be residue. Wash them with the pants you were wearing, pockets out."

What can I say? I read a lot.

"Do you have any drugs in your apartment?" I asked.

"No."

"Are you sure?" I knew I sounded motherly but I didn't care.

"No!"

I wanted to believe him. "If you do, get rid of them. And if you're really worried, why don't you talk to Olivia?" Olivia was the director of our program and Luke's close friend. She hadn't fired him when she found out he'd skipped all those instruction hours.

"No, Poppe. Promise me you won't tell her. Don't say a word."

Down the Rabbit Hole

The next day, Luke spiraled farther down the rabbit hole. He panicked that the cocaine couple were going to blackmail him, which struck me as preposterous. He thought they had someone watching him, ready to pounce when he stepped on campus to return his work computer. He worried that someone would come for him at the bank when he went to get his final paycheck or at the airport just as he was about to board his plane. I reassured him, saying it would cost too much to have someone watch him 24/7. I teased that he wasn't rich enough to watch. I joked that he was being paranoid. I lied, saying everything would be okay.

*

The following day there was a lost food delivery boy roaming the corridor on our floor. I went to Luke's, thinking he might not have heard a timid knock on his door if he were in the inflatable kiddie pool on his balcony. We'd lazed many an hour along the pool's cushioned edge, cooling our feet in the dandelion afternoons. When Luke answered his front door, he opened it just far enough to turtle his head through the doorway. His head and face were freshly shaved, but he looked clammy. His eyes darted back and forth along the length of the hall.

I gestured to the delivery boy behind me. "Did you order food?"

"Nah." When Luke spoke, it was more slush than sound.

I turned to the delivery boy and shrugged my shoulders, "Sorry."

The delivery boy checked his ticket and then took off down the stairs.

I turned back to Luke. "Are we're still on for tonight?" I was supposed to pick him up for his going away party at our friend Miran's house.

"Yeah. Yeah."

But when I returned that evening, he told me he wasn't coming. Instead, he urged me to go on his behalf and make his apologies. I agreed on the condition that he give me his extra set of keys so that I could check on him afterwards. I returned a few hours later with Gatorade and potato chips to find his living room windows shut, and the aircon turned off, the apartment hot and stuffy with June's heat. Luke sat cross-legged on his couch, cocooned in a blanket, staring at the TV. Later, my mind would thumb back and forth over that moment, realizing too late what I had seen.

I tried to keep it light. "I told everyone you were pale and not feeling great, and let them fill in the blanks for themselves A lot of people came up with food poisoning." Our boss Olivia had been at the party. Since I was an unpracticed liar and the only single person at a party full of couples, I had spent most of the evening playing with Miran's eight-year-old daughter and avoiding my boss. "Your friends think you're shitting your brains out," I sing-songed and handed him the Gatorade.

"Shh. They've bugged my apartment—"

For a moment I thought he was putting me on. "What they?"

"I've been hearing voices."

"When? Tonight? Before the party? That was me, listening to *DemocracyNow!* while I was taking a shower." I could have an entire conversation with Luke through our shared bathroom wall.

"Other voices."

"People are back from the Eid break to start the summer term. Tre and her son are back." Tre and her son lived above me, but she often complained about Luke's loud music.

Luke's eyes bugged. "Poppe, are you sure? Oh man, oh man, oh man. Last night, in the middle of the night," Luke pressed his lips together and shook his head, "I think I took a kitchen knife upstairs. You need to go and check on them."

I got that skin-crawl feeling. "You think or you know?"

"I don't know."

Logic fought panic and won. "Wait. I saw Tre today, coming back from Carrefour."

"Are you sure?"

"Yeah, I helped her with her bags."

I didn't know how to understand Luke's behavior because I'd never seen him unhinged or possibly dangerous. Before I had gone to the party, I'd leveled with Miran about what was going on, but Miran didn't use drugs either and naively thought the cocaine Luke had snorted on Tuesday needed to work through his system. Today was Friday.

Luke and I sat in silence, with me watching Luke watch the TV. I thought about how I hadn't liked him when we first met. How he had plopped down into the empty airplane seat next to me, drunk, and talked at me, revealing how he had been in jail in Korea for growing marijuana plants in his apartment, how Kurdistan was a fresh start. How I realized we were employed at the same school, but I still sent him back to his seat, not caring what he told our new colleagues. How he sidled up to me as we deplaned in Istanbul for the long layover, put his arm around my waist, and said, "Let's see about finding you a shower," and my curt, clear, impolite response. We had become friends slowly, carefully, Luke teaching me how to unworry and me giving him I don't know what. I sat in his moist living room, quietly resenting him. I didn't consider him one of my closest friends, wasn't sure how much we'd stay in contact once he left, and suspected I was dealing with him by default because most of his party posse had left for summer break. I was sweaty and impatient and frustrated. I didn't understand what was happening to him and I didn't know how to help him.

"I want to go to the US consulate tomorrow." Luke said, not looking at me.

"That is such a bad idea. What are you going to say? 'I did drugs with this couple and now they're after me.'? You'll be the one who gets in trouble." I doubted the university would risk its reputation to bail a using teacher out. "Why don't you sleep in my apartment if you feel unsafe here?"

"I don't want to put you in danger." He kept his eyes glued to the TV.

His paranoia was suffocating.

*

The next morning, I heard something in the hallway outside my front door. It was Luke, darkening my doorway.

"I knocked. Why didn't you answer?" he demanded. He was holding his suitcase and a backpack.

It was too early for crazy. The long, bony fingers of Luke's behavior had poked my conscience all night. When I awoke a little while before, I called a mutual friend who used to work for the university and lived life like he had died more than once. He said he would call Luke later but never did. "I didn't hear you. I was peeing."

Luke came in and paced the length of my entry way. Rubbing the top of his head, he rattled off his regrets: the half-truths and infidelities and downright betrayals. I wanted to plug my ears because there are some things you can't un-hear, and I didn't want to lower my opinion of him. Tamping down my judgment, I reminded myself of my own shortcomings and simply listened. Luke said he was on his way to a hotel to call his friends in the States.

"Why do you have to go to a hotel to phone them? Phone from your apartment."

"I think they bugged my apartment."

Inwardly, I rolled my eyes and then tried to awaken my patience. "There is no they." My patience slept on. "Fine. Phone them from here."

Luke's eyes narrowed. "They might have gotten to you too."

I spoke in a carefully measured tone. "No one has gotten to me." I nodded my head until Luke was nodding with me. "You can have the living room, and I'll go into my bedroom."

He side-eyed me. "Have you left your apartment?"

"No. I've been here all week."

Luke slid his backpack from his shoulder.

"Except for the gym."

His backpack dangled. "That's enough time."

For what, I wanted to scream, ready for him to leave. "No one has been here." I spoke deliberately, as if beading each word on a string.

He reached into his backpack and handed me a book. "Give this to Olivia."

It was his recipe book. Luke used to cook in his parents' restaurant before they closed up shop and traded the US for Korea. My mind flashed to the family dinner we had had the month before: Luke, cooking; all of us sprinkled around the kitchen, holding greedy plates. "Give the book to Olivia yourself. You're not leaving for a few days." My skin pricked. "Why are you going to a hotel? You're not—you're not thinking of killing yourself, are you?"

"No,...no! But Al, that's not a bad idea."

"Luke, you're scaring me. Tell me you won't do anything stupid."

We get so desperate for what we want to hear.

*

10:28 AM

> There are two men standing in the hallway outside my door

The text message was from Luke. I had talked him out of going to a hotel but failed to convince him to stay in my apartment. He had gone back to his, and I was prepping for the start of the new term. Reading his message, I got that needle-belly feeling. What if he was telling the truth? Psyching myself up, I rushed into the hallway, but no one was there.

> I just checked the hallway. No one's there or in the stairwell

I berated myself for getting sucked into his vortex of paranoia. Needing to feel in control, I ran some errands. When I returned, there was another message.

11:08 AM

> It's not safe. Dont go outside

11:24 AM

> I just got back from the store. Outside is fine

> 11:36 AM
>
> Do you want my Kindle? I got the new Ferlinghetti. I can bring it over

> No. Can't Concentrate

> Netflix?

> No. Might try to sleep

> Want to go to the hotel pool? Leaving in about an hour

> No. Do you really have to?

I was relieved he had said no. The semester was to start the next day, and I couldn't wait to turn my brain off and lay out in the sun.

> Miran called me. He's trying to get ahold of you

> I'll call him

As I was leaving, I thought about knocking on Luke's door, but I didn't want to waste thirty minutes of sun time listening to go-nowhere psycho-babble. Later, I would never feel so bad about being me. While I was watching the elevator numbers light up in descending order, Luke was wrapping a garden hose around his waist before he rappelled off his seventh-floor balcony. As I left the front entrance, he hit a small patch of grass on the back side of the building.

The Impossible Do-Over

Severe head injury. Severe chest injury. Holocranial fracture. Spinal cord injury. Two broken legs. One fractured arm. Respiratory failure. On a stabilization table in a chaotic emergency room in a Kurdish hospital, Luke flatlined twice before he died.

*

Because I had invited my former roommate to the pool, our friends knew where to find me. Three pairs of feet carried three worried faces over a patch of manicured fake grass to where I lazed in a lounge chair. There were marshmallow words cushioning the cut of emotional pain against the haze of beer-induced sleepiness and frustrated upheaval. In the nightmare unreal of this day, I threw some money under a bottle, threw my dress over my bathing suit, threw myself into Miran's car, and tried not to throw up on the way to the hospital. When we got to there, I glimpsed Luke on a gurney, his track-suited legs oddly bent, his slight frame attached to machines. He looked smaller, less like a thirty-six-year-old man and more like a broken, wooden boy-doll. I remembered a fireman's description of his buddy after the Twin Towers fell on 9/11: "His wife wanted to know if he had suffered. How do I tell her the only thing holding his body together was his [fireman's] suit?" We get so desperate for what we want to hear.

This is my last image of Luke, for I was ushered away from his body and not allowed near him again "for my own good" but without my say. I wanted him to know I was nearby, that I hadn't abandoned him. In the short, long hours that followed, there were many questions to which I alone had answers, except for one. Why hadn't I told university authorities what was going on?

*

> *Everybody: Why didn't you tell the university what was going one?*
> *Me: I promised Luke I wouldn't.*
> *Everybody: You should have told us. We would have been able to do something.*
> *Me: I promised Luke I wouldn't.*
> *Everybody: If you had told us, we could have saved him.*
> *I open and close my mouth, a caught fish.*

*

I didn't say that I had told two people who work or used to work for the university and that telling hadn't saved Luke. Miran had asked me to keep his name out of the story. As a local, he could not afford to have his family's name linked to a scandal.

The following is a series of irreversible events, rewound: A security guard for our compound called the building manager after seeing a body fall and hit the grass below. Luke scaled the outside of the building using a garden hose. Luke placed his backpack containing his passport, wallet with several thousand dollars, and phone—but no apartment keys—near his balcony railing. Luke locked his apartment door from the inside. Luke called the university's head of security claiming someone was trying to kill him. Luke gave me the extra set of keys to his apartment.

Fast forward. Luke died. Because I had the set of keys which should have been turned in when his roommate left, and no keys were found on Luke's body, and he had claimed someone was trying to kill him, I was taken to the Asayish, Kurdistan's special security police, for questioning.

*

I heard he was pushed.
I heard he jumped.
I heard he was nervous about leaving.
I can't believe he's gone.
I heard the university asked for blood donations.
I heard the hospital didn't have enough of his blood type, and that's why he died.
I miss him.
I heard the university isn't going to pay to ship the body back.
I heard his brother had to start a GoFundMe.
I heard the university is paying, and the brother is hustling the university for money.
It's so quiet here without him.
I heard the brother wants the body shipped to him in the US.
I heard the parents want the body shipped to them in Korea.
I heard the university can't ship the body back until the police say so.
The State Department isn't saying much.
I heard he was trying to climb down from his balcony.
I heard he was trying to climb up from the sixth floor.
I heard the Asayish are involved.

*

Even though the Asayish had taken my written statement on two separate occasions, I was again pulled out of my class to talk to them. The woman who had given Luke the drugs had made them; the Asayish had found a lab in her home. She and her husband were from Pakistan, a country whose illegal drug trade generates billions of dollars as opiates, cannabis, ecstasy, and cocaine seep through Pakistan's long, porous border with Iran and into Kurdistan. The Asayish wanted me to identify the woman who'd given Luke the drugs even though I'd told them I couldn't. I hadn't taken a good enough look at her face. All I remembered were those yoga pants.

The sun was high as the university's head of security, a translator, and I were escorted through a maze of low cement buildings in a police compound. We were brought into a building bordering a courtyard and led through a suffocating hallway to an important somebody's office. The room was large and air-conditioned, with two sofas and some chairs forming a U along its perimeter. At the top of the U sat a man in a suit behind a large desk. Beside him was a mini fridge. Many men, soldiers in military uniforms and civilians in pressed, collared-shirts, sat or stood as space dictated. Their colognes mingled in the recycled air. The men in the room were carefully not looking at me as they spoke about me to the translator, who occasionally clarified a point about my written statement with me in English and then reported back to the men in Kurdish. Because I could not follow their conversation, I wondered who believed my statement, believed that I didn't use drugs, believed that I had done what I could to prevent Luke's death. When the translator was directed to move from the sofa we were sharing to the sofa on the opposite side of the room, my stomach slalomed.

The office door opened, ushering in a blast of sand-roasted heat and a middle-aged woman. She looked vaguely familiar. For a moment, I thought she was the actress who had played an FBI agent on *The Blacklist*. The woman sat down next to me on the sofa, and we observed each other in the static quiet. A uniformed soldier spoke, and the woman next to me moved across the room to sit next to my translator. Everyone watched the woman and I look at each other from opposite sides of the room before she was dismissed. I shot my translator a WTF? look and received a shoulder shrug response. After another flurry of Kurdish, the university's head of security, my translator, and I were led outside and made to wait in the courtyard. I was told that the woman who had come into the room was the Pakistani woman who had given Luke the drugs, and that she had confirmed I had been sitting at the bar with Luke when he bummed a cigarette. Without my prior knowledge or consent, I had just participated in an eyewitness identification process called a show-up, with no effort made to protect my identity.

Inside me, anger, fear, and guilt slugged it out with no real winner. I wanted to know how big the Pakistanis' home lab was, did they work alone or were they part of a larger drug trade? Did I have a target on my back? Was I safe? Did I deserve to be safe after what had happened to Luke?

I wanted to yell at the head of security for disrespecting my agency, but I didn't. I had already told him I couldn't positively identify the woman whom Luke had met, nor had I been there when she had given him the drugs. Not only was the head of security one of the most powerful people at the university, let alone the Sulaimaniyah region because his brother had been martyred saving the president of Iraq's life, but the head of security blamed me for Luke's death and wanted me fired. He said I should have told them.

Should haves.

There's a line in Lanford Wilson's play *Burn This*, where the character Pale, furious and gnawed with grief after the death of his brother, says the world is going down the toilet on "I'm sorrys." The world excuses itself with "should haves." Shifts blame with reproach. Grants mea cupla reprieves.

The head of security could have acted on Luke's phone calls when Luke reported that someone was trying to kill him the night of his party, but to my knowledge, the head of security didn't. Perhaps he didn't hear Luke's messages because it was late at night when Luke called him, but Luke fell shortly before 1 pm the next day. No one investigated anything until after Luke had died.

A man in a tan shirt with three small children in tow stared at me as they walked through the courtyard past us and into the building we had just exited.

Time slowed.

The tan-shirted man and two of the three children exited the building, lingering just outside its entrance. The Pakistani woman stood in the doorway, holding their smallest child to her chest, the sun beating against her face, casting half-moons of shadow under her eyes. Over the toddler's shoulder, she looked at me with anger and fear; dread and regret. I wondered about her take-backs: first high, first deal, first batch. Going to that bar that night. Giving Luke a cigarette. Issuing the invitation. I imagined the scene in her plush house; Luke sitting with her in a pastel-colored living room scented with rose water, she offering him coke on a silver tray, he cutting it with his ID cards. Luke lowering his head to the tray. Freeze frame. The impossible do-over.

Swaying gently, the Pakistani woman clung to the toddler in her arms, cooing into his ear, peppering fervent kisses on his cheek, inhaling his smell. Time stretched. The tan-shirted man pulled the toddler from his mother's arms as a security officer led the Pakistani woman from her patch of sunlight into the building's dark.

"Justice" is swift in Kurdistan. Within days, I was told the woman had been imprisoned, the woman and her husband had been imprisoned, the woman and her husband had been disappeared, they had been deported, she had been imprisoned and he had been deported. No one mentioned the home lab. No one mentioned if the cocaine Luke had snorted had been cut with something else. No one mentioned a forensic toxicology report. No one mentioned the possibility that a tainted drug supply could kill other young people in our city. No one mentioned if the husband and wife worked alone or were part of something bigger. No one mentioned the children. I thought about Luke, left on his own before he was old enough to drive, and I added motherless children to the collateral damage ledger.

A lot of people wished I had told Olivia about the drugs. Many people wished Luke had gotten on a plane the moment his term ended instead of waiting until after the Eid holiday. Some people wished the university's head of security had immediately responded when Luke called him, saying people were after him. A few people wished Luke hadn't snuck into the apartment below his to drink the owner's alcohol, which exacerbated his drug-induced paranoia. Those who knew wished Luke had told those who didn't that he had had a drug-induced psychotic break in high school. One person wished she had sacrificed some sun time and knocked on Luke's door once more. I wish for all of the above.

Nine

Naples, Italy 2019

Tethered

I lifted my head from the dark asphalt and pushed myself onto my elbow. The right side of my body throbbed. The skin on my back screamed with fire; blood was streaming from the right side of my head and along my right elbow. Looking down, I saw my own naked breasts. My breath curved like a question. What had happened to my dress? Shame pushed out panic as I registered an older couple coming towards me from across the Neapolitan street. *Must cover my breasts. Must cover my breasts!* I looked for the straps which had tied my halter dress around my neck. They were hanging near my stomach. Tilting my head so the blood would run into my hair and not in my eyes, I pulled them up, but one strap was too short while the other had a large knot and was too long.

I needed a moment.

Images recollected and arranged. A man passing on a motorcycle had snatched my handbag, but he hadn't bargained for it being secured around my wrist. To be fair, I hadn't registered that I was being robbed. At first, I thought my bag had snagged his handlebar and I was about to shout my apology when he took off, taking me down to the ground. The left side of my body slammed to the ground with the initial impact. As the mugger sped down the moderately-trafficked street, I was banged onto my back. Being dragged along the pavement lacerated my back and shoulders and shore through the straps of my dress. As I was being dragged and skinned, I saw the handle which held the handbag to my right wrist tear a little. The keys to my Airbnb, my phone, and my only credit card were in it. I turned, so my left hand could gain purchase on the body of the bag, and my right hand, strangled in the strap, clawed upward. Now, the right side of my body was suffering the friction of being pulled along the street, but I had a firm grip on my bag. The purse-snatcher must have realized I wasn't letting go, so he did and gunned it. That's when my head smacked the pavement.

I held the halter's triangles of cloth to my breasts as the older couple reached me. I loved this orange, hot pink, and violet psychedelic-patterned piece of '70s era nostalgia. I had bought it at a vintage shop to celebrate getting my first job in Kurdistan, Iraq almost ten years earlier. This dress had gone wine tasing in West Jerusalem, to rock concerts in New York City, to art shows in Leipzig, to art residencies outside Barcelona and Cadiz, and to artistic heaven at Versailles. It had climbed ruins in Lebanon, learned Spanish in Seville, danced imitation flamenco at *la feria* in Puerto de Santa María, toured coffee plantations in Boquete, Panama, researched the Srebrenica Genocide in Sarajevo, released fire lanterns on New Year's Eve in Chiang Mai, drunk cheap bubbly while waiting for the Eiffel Tower to light up, done a book reading in Chicago, and nudged me to break up with a jealous, controlling boyfriend who thought the dress was too sexy for Cartagena. This dress was more than a dress. It was a Wonder Twins cape of super powers, ready to activate confidence with a single wear. In my fledgling Italian and tears, I begged the woman to tie it back around my neck while her partner called an ambulance.

I had gone to Italy to take refuge after Luke died. He had snorted some possibly skunked cocaine made in a homemade lab in the house of a Pakistani couple in Kurdistan, and later, he fell off the balcony of his apartment while trying to repel down the side of our building using a garden hose. Kurdistan's special police called me in for a show-up, an identification process where the person of interest and the witness see each other face to face. Because the show-up had led to the shutdown of the lab and the disappearance of the Pakistani woman, I didn't know if I had a target on my back. There were few foreigners in the Kurdish city where I lived, and the university where I taught had just used my image in a promotional video splashed across Facebook and Instagram. Hijacked by grief, fear, and fatigued, I flew to Italy to get a grip after my summer teaching term ended. I wanted to visit Naples and Sicily, home to my mother's side of the family, to see if either place was somewhere I, too, could call home.

After Luke died, the university's head of security showed me a restaurant's security camera footage of Luke and a woman sitting at the bar to see if I could identify her. The footage was an over-the-shoulder shot from behind the woman, who was dressed in a vintage turquoise Mexican wedding dress, hanging insouciantly off one shoulder. I told the head of security I couldn't identify the woman as I silently judged her for showing that much skin. Then, I realized she was me. Visiting the United States after living in places where you can't take electricity or running water for granted, where cholera outbreaks rob the city of all lettuce, and where your students are displaced or their families live in displacement camps feels a bit like that. I am on the outside looking in, not always recognizing what I see.

Were the houses in the US always so big? Did supermarkets always carry so many kinds of cereal? Did every driveway always have two or more vehicles parked in it? I judge the excess even as I am guilty of it. After all, the closet in the spare bedroom where I store my belongings is bursting with my collection of specialty frocks, some of which still bear tags, and yet, the collection grows. I can take myself out of US culture but I can't take all of US culture out of me.

What ties a person to a place? What un-ties them?

Behind closed eyes, I see my father sitting on the newspaper-covered foyer floor of our modest, middle-class, suburban Chicago home on Lilac Way. He is tall and I am small, but when he sits on the floor, we are almost the same height. Mom is wrangling my sisters for Sunday mass as Dad cleans and polishes his dress shoes for the work week ahead, and I stand by the front door, watching. He works fastidiously, using first a brush and then a soft cloth, which live together in a wooden box with a foot rest handle. This is his work ethic, brought from his home country to his now-home country and gifted to me to take wherever I go. Although he never quite lost his German accent nor his taste for liverwurst, German pickles, marzipan, and Dominostein, he considered himself American, not German, and he never wanted to live anywhere but the United States.

Hasan, a former student, was living in the university's dormitory in Sulaimaniyah in 2014 when ISIS captured his home town of Heet. He told me how his father had to flee Heet because he worked as an Anbar province coordinator for the United Nations, and ISIS kept a very detailed data base of residents in its captured territories. If ISIS had discovered Hasan's father's side hustle, he would have been executed. Leaving behind the family compound, which had taken Hasan's father thirteen years to build, Hasan's father hid whatever money and gold jewelry he could fit into his pockets so ISIS would not suspect he was fleeing and held his breath as he passed through checkpoints. He made it first to Baghdad and finally to Sulaimaniyah, where he rebuilt his life. Hasan's father remarried and taught English in the Kurdish public schools until the day he received a notice from the Iraqi government saying he had to return to Heet or risk losing a government subsidy upon which he and his second wife relied. Although the couple did not want to return, they did and found that ISIS had burnt the family compound to the ground.

The Merriam-Webster dictionary definition of dispossessed is "deprived of home, possessions and security." After his university graduation, Hasan had to leave Sulaimaniyah, a place where he had a home, possessions, and security, to return to Heet, a place where the family home had been destroyed, none of his possessions remained, and due to ongoing ISIS activity in the Anbar province, definitely lacked security. He had tears in his eyes when he told me, "I wake up and go onto the balcony [in his Sulaimaniyah apartment], and it is safe. The street is quiet. There isn't gunfire. In the distance, I see the mountains. Why would I want to leave? There is nothing to go back for."

I have taught many dispossessed students. In a cohort of adult learners at the university's professional development institute, a forty-something female painter named Narin, married but childless, recalled fleeing Mosul as ISIS took over her city. Narin and a nephew escaped on foot to the autonomous region of Kurdistan where "I collapsed on the ground in front of the first house I saw." Narin told me strangers took her and her nephew in, housing and feeding them until they felt strong enough to continue to Sulaimaniyah, where Narin's sister lived. Later, Narin would confide that her husband had been disappeared as ISIS sieged Mosul, that she had paid thousands of dollars to fixers who said they knew where he was and could rescue him. Because they hadn't, she wanted to return and look for him herself despite the danger. The last time I saw her was in the hair dye aisle of a local supermarket. She would soon be returning to Mosul to look for her husband or at least for some answers because "as you know Alex, my husband was one of Saddam's cousins." Mosul had not yet been liberated from ISIS. I never saw her again.

Yazidis, an ethno-religious minority living in northern Iraq, were attacked by ISIS at Sinjar Mountain in 2014. ISIS committed mass murder of Yazidi men, forced religious conversions on those who were not slaughtered, and abducted and enslaved thousands of Yazidi women and girls. Yazidi women were repeatedly raped, bought and sold at human sex slave markets, and forced to marry ISIS fighters. (Two of my former colleagues from the international school later worked with Yazda, an organization that documents and supports Yazidi victims of genocide and enslavement.) The Kurdistan Workers' Party (PKK), a militant Kurdish separatist group, established a defense line around Mount Sinjar and opened a safe corridor for Yazidis fleeing ISIS. The private university where I worked sponsored scholarships for several Yazidis students, who lived in the dorms while their family members lived in internally displaced person (IDP) camps on the opposite side of the Kurdish region near Sinjar.

Despite the atrocities my Yazidi students had experienced, they hadn't hardened. During our term together, the electricity on our campus mysteriously went out every day from about 4 pm to 11 pm while the public university across the street remained fully lit up. It was winter. The students in the dorms were cold, and they couldn't cook food or do homework until the power went back on. The founder of our university had recently been elected the president of Iraq, partly on the strength of his anti-corruption reputation. Some speculated our campus's power failure was payback for the president not granting political favors based on *wasta*.

I reasoned that some of my Yazidi scholarship students might not have extra money to go out to eat while the power was off, so I wrote them letters sharing one of my father's Berlin stories. The American employer of one of my grandmother's friends had sent care packages to my grandmother and father in Berlin throughout

World War II although the employer did not know them personally. My father credited those packages for his and his mother's survival. I wrapped the letters around some cash and put them in envelopes. The next day, assuring my students that they were not in trouble, I asked them to meet me after class and gave them the letters with strict orders not to open them until they returned to their dorm rooms. The following day, Mazen, their unofficial spokesperson, asked to "see me after class" with the promise "that I was not in trouble." Once we were gathered, they thanked me for the letters, which, according to Bassim, another student, "was the real gift" and tried to return the money. I told them I respected them too much to cook for them, and I was worried that they couldn't have dinner when the electricity was out. We argued back and forth about taking support when it is offered, about kindness versus charity, and about creating the kind world in which we wanted to live. My students finally agreed to take the money but assured me they would only use it if they "really needed it" or if they saw someone in the dorms who did. They wished to send the rest to their families who were living in the camps.

Despite or perhaps due to growing up within so much violence, there is a specific sweetness to the students I have taught in the Middle East, be they Kurdish, Arabic, Palestinian, Syrian, or Yazidi. Many of my twenty-something students were tweens or younger during the 2003 US-led invasion. Hasan remembered US soldiers sometimes removing their gloves to shake hands with his father before a house-to-house search or sometimes kicking in the front door. People in his hometown of Heet started leaving their front doors unlocked and ajar when they went to bed at night so that the front doors wouldn't get kicked in or broken down during house raids.

Hasan told me about a house search that happened when he

was eleven years old. US soldiers sat him, his two older brothers, their father, some uncles, and a grandfather all in a row, like birds on a clothes line, in front of their living room wall. Through the open front door trailed the cooing of twilight bugs beguiling one another before they spread their wings and took flight. A military interpreter sitting next to Hasan magicked one of the US soldier's funny-sounding words into a question, "What do you know about the bombs on the street?"

No one had the answer.

The interpreter didn't need to translate the soldier's punches. Violence was the same in any language.

"Shut up, you fat kid," the soldier yelled as he took a crying Hasan into another part of the house to be interrogated. Again, the soldier asked Hasan what he knew about the bomb that had been planted one hundred meters from Hasan's house.

Hasan thought this was the moment to be brave. "If you want information, come get it yourself."

Smothering a smile, the interpreter mistranslated Hasan's words. In response, the soldier threatened to take Hasan to prison if he didn't talk.

"If you do that," Hasan reasoned, "you will be the terrorist."

During another house search, the men in Hasan's family were lined up in the courtyard and beaten after soldiers found Hasan's father's army rifle and license. Seeing the look on my face, Hasan tried to reassure me, "Pain is temporary. Something else will take its place."

"How do you not hate Americans?" I asked.

Hasan thought about it for a moment. "They're not the main reason for the destruction of Iraq. The people didn't stand together." He was referring to the spiral of sectarian violence that began in 2006 when Al-Qaeda in Iraq bombed the Al-Aksari

Shrine in Samarra, one of the holiest sites for Shia Islam. This set off a wave of Shia reprisals towards Sunnis, which led to Sunni counterattacks. Hasan said that when the US army invaded, the Shia flourished and started executing anyone named Omar, which is a typical Sunni name. In 2006, when Hasan's brother went to university in Baghdad, he had two identification cards: one Sunni, one Shia. Hasan told me, "You get used to going around and maybe being blown up. You don't give up details about family. You learn to lie. You learn to be Shiite with strangers."

Tall, medium built, with close cropped hair and five-day growth sideburns connecting to his goatee, Othman, one of my students from the professional development institute, could model for a luxury car ad if he traded his hoodie for a suit. Othman is from Basra, one of the first cities to fall during the 2003 invasion. When he was eight years old, he watched as his father and uncles pointed shotguns out the windows of their home to defend themselves from a Shia militia in the street. The two sides exchanged fire, which drew the attention of some British soldiers on patrol in a tank. The tank entered their street, and the soldiers told everyone to drop their weapons or they would shoot. The British soldiers seized the guns, put the guns in a car, ran over the car with the tank, and took the Shia militia into custody. Othman told me that if the tank hadn't shown up, the militia probably would have killed them. Othman's father and uncles were spared when his father explained he was a doctor in the Iraqi army and showed his badge. At that time, the US army was creating a new Iraqi army in Baghdad, so the British army arranged for Othman's father to join the new force.

Othman and his family move to a mixed Sunni and Shia neighborhood in Baghdad. In 2006, when Othman was twelve years old, sectarian violence again flared. As the summer sun sizzled the cracked streets like a giant, open pit frying pan, masked gunman set up roadblocks in mixed neighborhoods, checked identification cards, and murdered people with a Sunni name. Othman is Sunni. One day, a Sunni neighbor married to a Shia woman jumped over the low stone wall separating their house from Othman's to warn Othman and his family: *The Shia are coming.*

What would you grab if you had five minutes to leave your life?

Othman shook his head as he told me that his last image of Baghdad was a rocket landing a few houses down from his.

Salim, a student from Tikrit, told me how US forces killed his aunt and her husband in front of the family. Again, there was a house search. Because many of the men were out when the soldiers arrived, the women feared the soldiers might take things of value. The women stuffed their gold and jewelry into their pockets as the search began. Fearing someone might have a bomb, a soldier demanded to know what Salim's aunt had put in her pockets. When she did not respond, the soldier roughly seized her arm as her husband was arriving home. He rushed the soldier to defend his wife's honor. The soldier shot and killed them both.

Instead of harboring resentment towards me, an American, the students offer to carry my books or my computer when they see me on campus. They tell me they love me, and they don't mean it in a sexual way, and they are not embarrassed to say it. They blow me parade float kisses from across the campus. They run up to hug me when they see me on quad. They organize birthday cakes and gather other former students together so everyone can enter my classroom singing as they slip a paper crown on my head and light some candles. They bring in muscle-relaxing cream when I hobble around the classroom with a bad back. They send me jokes on WhatsApp. They Facebook message me when they hear I am ill. They Facebook message me after President Trump announces the Muslim travel ban because they worry I may not be able to return to the US. They Facebook message me when they decide to become teachers or earn advanced degrees in English literature. They Facebook message me to tell me they've completed med school abroad and thank me for showing them an alternative way for women to live. Excited grooms send wedding photos. Proud fathers send baby pictures. They Facebook message me to send prayers when my father is ill. They pray for my mother. They message me every day as my father hangs on in an intensive care unit in a hospital in a country which broke theirs.

My brush with Italian violence didn't sweeten me; it steeled me. Before the motorcyclist snatched my bag, I had been devasted by heartbreak. I had not only lost Luke, but I had also been left by a man I loved. Because being dumped happened at the same time Luke died, the two losses were bound together for me. I couldn't speak to or about my ex without choking up. Once I realized I was about to lose my handbag and that I could try to stop another loss from happening, something internal shifted. I became more muscle than mind. Turning onto my right side so I could get a better grip on the bag as the motorcyclist dragged me down the street was my Angelina Jolie action figure moment. I felt victorious, a phoenix rising, until the purse snatcher let go and my head smacked the pavement.

Lying eye-level with stubbed cigarette butts discarded in the gutter, blood running into my ear, moist and jungly, I thought about how people always say, "At least you have your health," when life sucker punches you. I idly wondered if I had a concussion but dismissed the idea because I didn't know anything about concussions. My vanity kicked in, urging me to check that all my teeth were still in my mouth. Luckily, no bones were broken. I was bruised and bloody and skinned; my back felt on fire, but I was otherwise intact. When my boss Olivia heard about the attempted bag grab, she joked that the bag snatcher "had picked the wrong woman" before adding the incident was a metaphor for how I live: "You don't let go. You'll fight." Her observation is too generous, for I have always been protected by the umbrella of safety my birth gifts (being born white in the US to a middle-class family) afford. I also have the opportunity to let go, to leave conflict and post-conflict zones whereas my students do not.

In the days following the attempted purse snatch, my ex and I exchanged messages during which my voice was even, my tone and language neutral. It was as though my mushy innards had morphed into bionic hardware beneath a skin veneer. The fear I felt after my head had smacked the pavement slow-thawed into a cool anger, which is different from the Viking anger I usually feel. My Viking anger centers in my heart; it is emotional and reactionary because what provokes it feels personal. My steeled anger centered in my groin; it was physical because it was the consequence of taking action. I had met aggression head on and prevented another loss. My walk morphed into a swagger.

Then my father died.

I want to add deprived of person to the definition of dispossessed. The loss of my father was an untethering. We're never too old to be little. The night he died, I slept with the bird puppets "Santa" had given me when I was a child and wept until I aged myself. Crying into their synthetic fur, I was a tumbleweed, alone and adrift in an uncertain world. I felt small because my father and I had argued on the way to the airport and were reluctant to hug each other at departures. That was the last time I saw him alive in person. In the aftermath of his death, I felt lost, like a child in feet pajamas who awakens from a nightmare and doesn't recognize anything in the dark. I wanted to be his daughter for a little while longer. This feeling, nebulous but encompassing, was an unknown land I was unprepared to navigate. Tipping on the tightrope between his presence and his absence, I couldn't take the next step. All around me, the air had turned to glue.

A few years ago, I wrote a piece for *Bust.com* about single women living longer than men and not having enough money to retire in the US. In it, I wrote about a phone call I had had with my parents, in which they asked me if I ever wanted to live full time in the US again, and my ambivalence towards that because I hadn't yet found myself by official societal standards of marriage, kids, and property ownership. The last line of the essay is this: "When these two old people {my mother and father} are gone, there'll be one less place to call home." To my surprise, in the space left by my father's absence, the US beckoned me, pulling taut, pulling tired, perhaps because he loved the US so much, and I wanted to hang on to him. I longed to hear his rough voice in my ear telling me to slow down or arguing for American exceptionalism. This was something to go back for, at least for a little while.

Bryan Mealer's excellent book, *All Things Must Fight to Live*, is an odyssey through the aftermath of war in the Congo, how everyday people make sense of their lives amidst the chaos and catastrophe of violent conflict. Because of my birth gifts, I have not had to make sense of a war-interrupted life. My father did; my students do. Some leave their homeland because staying is too hard. Others dig in because leaving is defeat. I wonder if home is simply a construct of choice; either the place we hang onto at all costs or the place that catches us after we let go.

Ten

Sulaimaniayh, Kurdistan, Iraq 2020-2021

Ode to WhatsApp

Dream shards splintered over my bed as the muffled beep of a message notification surfaced me from sleep. My bottom-left jaw reverberated with an icy, magnetic ache. Although I wore a nightguard, I had grinded my teeth hard enough to impact a tooth. Fingering darkness, I found my cell phone and checked WhatsApp before doing anything else. There were several melodramatic student pleas for help, including the one that had just pulled me from greasy sleep.

I checked the time—a bit after 4 am—and cursed genealogically. I hadn't fallen asleep until after 1 am because my roommate Kayla didn't use an indoor voice when teaching online, which she often did until after midnight. Since transferring to online instruction, text and voice messages ping-ponged between the students and me throughout the day and night, mocking traditional office hours. The same was true for Kayla. She taught from the living room because the Wi-Fi was spotty in her bedroom. I sequestered myself in my bedroom because Kayla was a cancer survivor, and I still used our building's mold-ridden gym. Neither of us were vaccinated. Caught in the first year of COVID-19 in Kurdistan, we were locked down, lodged in, and online, imparting skills and knowledge to university students with varying degrees of success.

I had flown back to Kurdistan in the third week of February 2020, preoccupied with US-Iran relations instead of thinking about the pandemic. In early January, the US had assassinated Iran's second most powerful person, Qasem Soleimani, in a drone strike at the Baghdad International Airport. Because General Soleimani had been on his way to meet Iraqi Prime Minister Adil Abdul-Mahdi, some people thought the general had been killed with Iraq's tacit complicity although Iraq protested the attack, saying it had undermined its national sovereignty. The Iraqi Parliament called for the expulsion of all foreign troops. What followed was an existential trinity of response: Iran vowed revenge, the US stated it would preemptively attack Iranian paramilitary troops it considered a threat in Iraq, and Iraqis worried its country would become the battleground for a proxy war. They were right. Iran bombed US bases in Kurdistan, but Iran's reprisal attack on the Ukraine International Airlines Flight 752 ended up quelling the escalation. The Islamic Revolutionary Guards Corp (IRGC) had mistaken the international passenger flight for an American cruise missile and shot it down, killing all 176 people onboard, most of whom were Iranians or Iranian diaspora returning to their adopted countries.

Meanwhile, COVID was beginning to Whac-A-Mole the world. As I touched down in Sulaymaniyah sans mask, all the passengers and crew aboard the Diamond Princess cruise ship were being quarantined off the coast of Japan and prevented from returning to the US for at least 14 days. Italy was becoming the global hotspot of infection, and the number of infected people next door to us in Iran was rising daily, a harbinger of the illness and tragedy to come. A popular border crossing between Iraq and Iran is about 60 miles away from Sulaimaniyah.

Being back in Sulaimaniyah felt like standing at the edge of a sink hole; it was only a matter of time until I fell in. As I watched people around the world hording toilet paper, I realized I didn't know how to prepare for COVID beyond buying a few extra six-packs of counterfeit bottled water. I focused on the starting term:

setting up my classroom, prepping a few weeks' worth of lessons, photocopying supplementary materials, and writing quizzes while watching the number of worldwide infections soar. Two days into the new term, admin sent the faculty home and told us to get ready to go online. I hadn't had enough time to learn all of my students' names, let alone connect with them as people. On February 25, the Kurdistan Regional Government (KRG) pro-actively sealed its border with Iran and announced an end to on-campus instruction region-wide.

Most of us had no idea how to teach online. We frantically translated in-person content, activities, and assignments into bite-sized, scaffolded modules and uploaded them to the university's learning management system, the portal students used to access instructional materials and upload assignments. We filmed each other doing engagement activities on our cell phones in between reading up on what faculty at Harvard, MIT, and the University of Nebraska were doing. Faculty were invited back to the campus for two days of training on the basics of online instruction and how to use Zoom before we were let go like freed lab mice, wildly scattering into parts unknown.

We were slightly better prepared for the upcoming challenges than our students. Because they hadn't grown up in a culture of self-directed learning, most students lacked the discipline to watch lectures on their own, take notes, work through PowerPoints, or do homework unless there was a teacher supervising them or assessing their output. Cheating was rampant. When we put stricter testing protocols in place, the students suffered us as nitwits, which felt quaint. In response, I built more project-based learning into my curriculum and made all my assessments rooted in critical thinking and long form production.

Compounding the difficulty of transitioning from in person

instruction to online learning was that Iraq lacked the necessary infrastructure. Reliable access to electricity was non-existent, power cuts were a daily occurrence (independent of COVID), and many parts of the country had limited internet access. When there wasn't any electricity, the students couldn't connect to the internet unless they had data packs, which were expensive for some. I had students who had been internally displaced within Iraq and were now studying online from their tents inside internally displaced person (IDP) camps instead of from dorm rooms. Some of my scholarship students did not have private generators in their homes.

Although adept with using their cell phones, most of my university-aged students lacked basic computer skills, which weren't usually taught in public primary or secondary schools, and most public schools didn't have computers for students to use. Most of our students didn't know how to use Microsoft Word or upload an assignment to Turnitin, an internet-based plagiarism checking website. Some had never used email and didn't know how to set up an account. They usually learned those skills during the first week of my academic writing course, which was always the most agonizing lecture of the term for both the students and me. Teaching them these basic tech skills online made me less likeable than a worker at the DMV.

Beyond my tinfoil-covered windows, the sun was pinking the mountain tops in a sherbet glow. I removed my mouth guard and tossed it hopefully in the direction of my desk in the fading dark. Then I condensed about four weeks' worth of lectures on essay structure, thesis statements, and cited evidence into a nine-minute WhatsApp voice message when I wanted to admonish the student for not doing the building block assignments that would have prepared him for the current task. Rubbing my jaw between responses, I answered the remaining messages in the order they appeared in my feed, inadvertently penalizing those who had asked the earliest. Finally, I left another message in the students' group chat to remind them not to contact me after midnight, which was useless. It was Ramadan, the religious month of fasting to celebrate the angel Gabriel revealing the Qur'an to the prophet Muhammad. Because many students observed Ramadan, they stayed up until *suhur*, the predawn meal, and then slept during the day. If they did homework, they usually started after *iftar*, the evening meal to break their fast and would work into the wee hours of the morning.

Initially, I was reluctant to use WhatsApp, an internet-based instant messaging platform, to communicate with students because I didn't want them to have my personal phone number. Cognizant of social customs in the Middle East, I wasn't sure how a Western, female teacher calling a single, early twenty-something male student might be perceived. I also didn't want to blur the line between teacher and student by using a mode of communication usually reserved for friends, a standard that perished like a protein-based diet for the carb-motivated.

I also knew the students were going to struggle. Since we were the first university to go online in the Kurdish region, the students couldn't ask their friends at other universities for guidance. My class was also their first exposure to thesis statements, evidence, in-text citations, Modern Language Association (MLA) citation format, and essay writing, which students find difficult under the best of circumstances. Because learning is relationship-driven, especially in the Middle East (A study presented at a Teachers of English to Speakers of Other Languages {TESOL} Arabia conference a few years ago found that students in the US think their academic success is the result of their own hard work whereas students in the Middle East think their academic success depends on their relationship with their teachers.), I relented and joined the WhatsApp chat group that a student named Dila had already created.

There were occasional backfires. Late one weekend night, a student messaged me about my blue eyes and how much he liked my voice. My roommate, Kayla, and I laughed at his clumsily inappropriate overture as we drank counterfeit gin and tonics and socially distanced on our pigeon-pooped balcony. (With the liquors stores closed due to COVID and Ramadan, we had to call our fixer, who drove Kayla to a private home where she picked up our alcohol orders out of someone's backroom window.) Watching moths throw themselves against the balcony glass door, we took bets on how long it would take him to realize his indiscretion. He messaged an apology late the next day, blaming his behavior on alcohol. I had to block another student whose demands blazed like a struck match because he would not stop calling me between 3 and 4 in the morning.

Becoming a member of the students' WhatsApp group jinned up our collective intimacy. Being a fly-on-the-WhatsApp-wall enabled me to judge the students' stress levels when the group chat dissolved into emoticons, especially a flurry of crying-with-tears faces or frogs. (I had no idea why frogs.) It was the equivalent of a dorm hall all-nighter, without the pajamas, junk food, and cigarettes. In those moments, I could jump on the app and re-explain directions and key concepts between brushing and flossing or give examples for the students who couldn't/hadn't looked at the teaching content posted to our learning management system.

As the students worked through what they had to do, they shared jokes, memes, and personal triumphs. A student named Balen shared a photo of *kulera,* a type of Kurdish flatbread he had learned to make in his training to become a baker. They texted my motivational sayings such as "Mistakes are proof you're trying," and "The learning is in the doing," to one another as they struggled through homework together. Conversely, an absence of activity could signal something was amiss, especially at night when they typically did their assignments. My initiating contact through the group chat with an innocuous, "You're really quiet. Everything OK?" was the WhatsApp equivalent of walking around a physical classroom and peering over students' shoulders as they tackled something new.

Video calling on WhatsApp shredded any remaining formality of the traditional student/teacher relationship. When I video-called a student to teach her how to attach a word doc to an email via her computer, I saw her without her hijab, which never would have happened in the classroom. She saw the puppets sitting on my bed behind me in the corner of my camera screen. When I voice-called a non-participatory student to ask why he wasn't answering the live video call, he said plainly, "Miss, I don't have any clothes on."

"Good choice [not to answer]," I fumbled, quickly glancing down at my own sleeveless attire. On campus, female teachers had to cover their shoulders and their knees, but this phone call was outside of Zoom teaching hours. Did I still have to follow the university's dress code in my bedroom?

With the breaking down of barriers came increased vulnerability. In an earlier writing task, Dila had talked about the pain of her father leaving their family for a second wife. I gained a visceral understanding of her life when I saw the bare walls of the cramped family room and heard her toddler brother nagging her to play in the background of her video chat. Was there enough space for her coming-of-age chaos, or did she have to hide her labyrinthine emotions under a bedroom pillow? As her non-English speaking, hijab-wearing mother insisted on meeting me, I watched Dila hold her breath in anticipation of my judgment. The strained expression on Dila's face as her mother came into the video frame, and the involuntary noises Dila made as she measured my reaction to her mother's religious blessings colonized me with a new ache.

Dila was the den mother of her cohort. She dutifully posted a snapshot of the week's schedule from our learning management system into the group chat every Sunday morning to keep her classmates on track. If the students had major assignments due in their academic reading class, she was the one who would ask me to adjust the academic writing schedule. Seeing her at home on a WhatsApp video call was like looking into a kaleidoscope. The bare walls, her hijab-wearing mother (Dila didn't wear the traditional head scarf.), her insistent brother, and her absent father were colored-glass pieces of information that fell together in a turn, creating a new picture.

I remembered how much I dreaded non-uniform days at my Catholic grade school. My clothes were mostly hand-me-downs, ill-fitting or just plain wrong. While my classmates wore jeans and skittles-colored striped cardigans, I was the eight-year-old in an out-of-fashion, hand-me-down green dress trimmed in white piping and pantyhose. Flash forward to early adulthood. I learned how to build boxes to compartmentalize the parts of me I didn't want anyone to see. Inevitably, those boxes would cave in, leaving my imperfections exposed, the image I wanted to project replaced by the reality that was. How small I felt when fully seen, how unprotected. With a mixture of pride and sadness, I realized how alike Dila and I were.

Dila's brother and mother exited the video chat, leaving just the two of us caught in the frame. My jaw opened and closed in anti-speech. I longed to tell Dila of the high esteem in which I held her, but to do so would have acknowledged her insecurity, and I wanted to pretend I hadn't seen it. Besides, Dila wasn't ready to accept that her private self was the bones on which her public self was built. The poverty, abandonment, and tradition that embarrassed her was also what made her a problem-solving, caretaking, natural leader. As an act of mercy, I cleared my throat and returned to business as usual.

Breakfast Wine

No. No. No! They were gone.

I refreshed my screen, wondering where all the Turkish Airline international flights out of Sulaimaniyah had gone. Only two days prior, Iraq had announced it would re-open its airports for international commercial travel. Until the international airports opened for commercial travel, US nationals who wished to leave the country had to pay thousands of dollars to take evacuation flights out of Erbil. Even if I had been willing to shell out that kind of money, I was teaching the summer term online, and the administration had forbidden our department from leaving Kurdistan at the risk of dismissal. Since I had resigned right before the pandemic kicked in and then rescinded my resignation when I saw the COVID writing on the wall, I felt grateful to be employed even as we suffered yet another salary cut.

When Iraq decided to open its airspace, we gained some unexpected leverage, mostly, I think, because our director, Olivia, wanted to go back to the States, and she was too valuable to the university to risk her quitting. After much back and forth within the administration, we received word that our department's faculty could leave if we wanted as long as we maintained our online teaching schedule. However, if we couldn't get back into the country when the new term started, say if the airports shut down again, we risked losing our jobs even though we would still be teaching online.

Kayla and I decided to chance it and leave. I was due a

contractual term off, having worked four terms in a row, and I wanted to see my family. Given the risks of being unvaccinated and immune-compromised because of her cancer, Kayla decided to take an unpaid leave of absence because admin would not let her department teach remotely from the US. We immediately began searching for flights out. I found mine on Turkish Airlines while Kayla went with Qatar Airlines. Before I booked the flight, I wanted to secure a short-term rental in Chicago, so I hadn't booked the Turkish flight when I'd found it. Now, there were no Turkish Airlines flights out of Sulaimaniyah to be had.

It had been a difficult summer. Once lauded by the World Health Organization (WHO) for its fast and efficient response to the pandemic, Kurdistan now had high intermittent COVID case counts. In response, we'd be locked down for a week or two at a time, save for pharmacies and bakeries, but not liquor stores. Travel between Kurdish provinces was also banned. Despite border closings, infections spread north from Baghdad and west from Iran as well as organically inside the Kurdish region. Meanwhile, world demand for oil plummeted, driving its price to record lows. Again, budget shortfalls plagued the Kurdistan Regional Government (KRG), crippling its ability to pay public sector employees, including doctors and nurses. The Ministry of Health didn't have enough ICU beds, oxygen tanks, blood, and ventilators while health care professionals didn't have enough personal protective equipment (PPE) or medicine. After months of not being paid their full salaries, health care professionals were threatening to strike.

COVID struck our virtual classrooms as students or their family members fell ill. Rasan, who studied online from Baghdad, where night curfews were in effect, missed a major assessment because he had to run out and find oxygen tanks to take to his mother who was sick with COVID in the hospital. Zahra, also in

Baghdad, became ill as she took care of both her COVID-infected parents. Hussein offered to keep Zahra up-to-date with content and assignments even though all the live lectures were recorded on Zoom and uploaded to the learning management system, and I emailed Zahra the daily PowerPoints, practice materials, and assignments. When Hussein WhatsApped me confessing he was afraid Zahra wouldn't recover, I suspected a budding romance. Even over Zoom, they seemed like two people who could spot each other in a crowd. When Hussein and Zahra thanked each other in their gratitude letters as part of a student learning project, my suspicions were confirmed. They got engaged shortly after the term ended.

Keeping the students organized as we created and administered makeup exams, major assessments, and assignments was harrying, but the lack of reliable information from the English language news sites and an absence of any information from the university regarding COVID testing, airport updates, and quarantine requirements upon return was maddening. Sitting at an outside table at an impromptu café set up by an entrepreneurial local in our compound, I eavesdropped on some Americans and Brits not affiliated with our university to glean information. They discussed how they were using *wasta* to get out.

The day came and went for the airports to open, yet ours remained closed to international commercial flights. The KRG justified the delay by saying it wanted to put COVID protocols in place. Among those protocols were a requirement for taxi drivers entering the airport to be COVID tested at a cost of $40, and passengers to be COVID tested at a cost of $80, as reported by *Rudaw*, a leading English language Kurdish news site. Our fixer, Sarmand, whose friend worked at the airport, said this was not true. Only passengers needed a COVID test, which had to be done at a coronavirus-designated hospital. Our university said nothing. I called a journalist friend who confirmed the news report. In the end, our fixer was right.

Kayla set up another WhatsApp group to share information for faculty looking to clear out, and over medicinal limoncello we discussed strategy. If we couldn't get back into the country, we didn't want to leave anything of value behind. Kayla wasn't sure she'd return, but I still had another year left on my contract. In the end, I decided to ship about half of my belongings home while Kayla bought extra luggage allowance for her flight. I didn't want people to think I was doing a runner, so I snuck my suitcases out the back exit of the building along the frying pan pavement to a shipping company, avoiding the taxi rink. Others, including Olivia, were also furtively packing and shipping while maintaining a façade of business as usual. Working throughout the next year as I finished my contract, I never saw Olivia in person again.

Our next hurdle was how to get a COVID test in time to fly. This was tricky for a few reasons. Besides not knowing where to go and how to negotiate the myriad of lines to stand in without a translator, we had to calculate layover times and time zone changes to make sure the test would still be valid at our destinations. We didn't know how long test results took to get. Leaving on a Saturday complicated the issue because testing labs weren't open on Fridays, a day of religious observance in the Middle East. If your flight was rerouted to Erbil, you'd need a COVID test taken in Erbil because allegedly the one taken in Sulaimaniyah wasn't considered valid. There was also the risk of receiving a false positive, which was happening often enough to be a concern. There was a rumor that one out of every four tests was automatically declared positive because the local labs didn't have the capacity to test all the samples. We never knew if this was true, but my co-teacher's husband lost his flight to the US due to a false positive. When he tested the next day, he received a negative result, but by the time he received the second result, his first flight had already taken off. Luckily, our fixer navigated us through the testing process, using his *wasta* in the testing lines and making sure our results were ready in time for our flights.

We needed masks. Kayla had an N-95 she had brought from the States, but Kaia, a fellow faculty and lockdown pod member with a legendary gummy collection she'd somehow snuck into the country, and I didn't. Masks were difficult to find in the stores, but once again, Sarmand had a connection. Face shields were a different story. Even Sarmand didn't have enough *wasta*. Kaia researched how to make face shields on YouTube, and over sticky Jack Daniels cinnamon whiskey, Kaia and I made face shields from plastic water bottles, strips of an old yoga mat, and yarn for the three of us. They looked ridiculous but were more comfortable than wearing a scuba mask, (Kaia had an extra for me), which was an alternative.

The way we supported one another as we readied to leave reminded me of Ukrainian *hromade*, which means a community self-organizing and working together for its mutual survival. Some trace *hromade's* cooperative spirit back to the 17th century Cossacks, who were big on self-governance. Others attribute Ukrainians' tradition of self-organization as a means of communal survival to the 1980s, when there weren't enough goods for the general public, and the 1990s, when the Soviet economy collapsed. Now, after being locked down together for almost six months, our *hromade* was coming to an end.

Looking back at our final lockdown days together, I see Kayla, Kaia and me in tableau on my bed. Kaia's lying on her back, and Kayla's curled like a pill bug with her head on a pillow. I was folded like a praying mantis with my elbows on the mattress and my knees on the floor. They had just returned from getting COVID-tested in preparation for their States-bound flights two days later. I was due to fly the following week. We were drinking cheap Australian chardonnay at 11 in the morning as the air conditioner above our heads blew cold, sour air, chewing our hair. Lemon spokes of sunlight pierced the tears in the tinfoil covering my bedroom windows and fell in irregular slashes along the faux wood floor. (Each spring, we dutifully taped tinfoil on our bedroom windows to reinforce the blinds against the menacing sun.)

We lounged in dorm room intimacy, suspended in the desultory laze of an unstructured morning, decompressing. Back in the US, our hometowns were eating themselves from the inside out in the wake of George Floyd's murder and lockdown measures. A former colleague's son had just committed suicide after the family returned from Kurdistan, and a few days prior, I attended his funeral on Zoom. Turkish Airlines started cancelling international commercial flights from our city again, and we worried that Qatar Airlines would do the same. Conspiracy theories that COVID was a Kurdish government ploy to avoid paying public sector salaries abounded. Locals stopped wearing masks or wore them cradling their chins like jockstraps, putting everyone at risk. Anxiety was a giant snowball gaining in intensity and speed as it rolled down a steep hill, lapping at our heels, threatening to avalanche us. We gave it the middle finger and cracked open a second bottle. We would never be this close again. We were frazzled. We were excited. We were scared.

Time evanesces and the years I have known Kayla accordion-fold into a coy hand fan. Bruised memories, unconjured but possessive, come at me, barking my heart and gut. My first Latina moment, baptized by Kayla on Lalazar's rooftop terrace as we excavated the types of stories that build a friendship. How our budding friendship got sheared under the weight of a cancer diagnosis and a lengthy respite in the US for treatment. When Kayla returned two years later, her generous smile, a shaggy hammock swinging between chandelier earrings, became a writhing snake of pain one night after her colostomy bag got blocked. How I had to invoke her middle name and promise to kick her curbside at the emergency room entrance if she would just let me take a taxi with her to the hospital. How acidic puke bags of bile smelled and how ineffectual apologies were to a taxi driver who didn't speak my language. How I lived up to the cultural stereotype of a tone-deaf American throwing lots of extra cash at a problem as I overtipped the driver. How Kayla's tortured grimace turned into a courtesan's pucker as the intravenous pain meds kicked in, and she flirted with the emergency room doctor.

Jump cut to Kayla teaching me the "Mahna-Mahnam" *Muppet Show* song with my puppets when we got the lockdown crazies. Jump cut to our first and only fight, induced by COVID and settled with Italian eggs and tears. Jump cut to Kayla's rolling suitcase, its wheels rumbling across the concrete walkway like a bowling ball on gravel. Time stretches, untamed and unsteady, until we are old ladies with rune faces, meeting on Facebook messenger to play the "Remember When" game. In the here and now, I heat with a red wasp of feeling. The moment flares like the sun setting fire to the horizon—beautiful to behold but impossible to contain.

Departure

I walked into the tiny room, handed over my purse, and stood in a vertical spread eagle. A hijab-wearing woman mapped my outstretched arms with her hands as her colleague searched the contents of my handbag. Female Kurdish airport security personnel were notorious for their invasive pat down procedures, especially when they searched between your legs, and this woman was living up to the reputation. Over my black leather skirt, she roughly cupped my mons pubis as her colleague twisted up a tube of my MAC lipstick to marvel at the color. I sucked in my breath and willed myself still as the security screener slipped her fingers beneath the cups of my underwire bra and yanked up. Before she set me free, she honked both my nipples while looking directly in my eyes and told me they were beautiful. I grabbed my purse and passed like a giraffe into the departures area.

Beyond the airport's glass walls, a charcoal morning prolonged night's illusion over the desolate runway. This was my last sun up in Kurdistan, the last time I'd hear the muezzin announce the mournful day break call to prayer. Back in 2019, Luke's death, waiting to see if a Pakistani drug maker had put a target on my back, losing a great love, and the Naples mugging, all happening in the span of two months, caused me to shove my emotions deep down, like a rock dropped in a well, so I could function. Back in the States on my term off in 2020, they had biled up, choking me with crying jags that curled me into a couch. I returned to the university to finish my contract in 2021, and now, as summer gave way to a new fall term, I was leaving for good. It was about time I learned how to sit with myself outside of a conflict zone.

With the far side of life approaching, I'd realized that despite my nomadic stirrings, I needed to learn how to stay put for my life to expand, and Kurdistan was not the place for me to drop anchor. I was headed to Chicago, a city I had spent my adulthood escaping, to begin anew on that cleat of discord between where I was going and where I needed to go, but I didn't know where that was yet. I had accepted a remote job working for a humanitarian aid organization and planned to spend some time exploring different cities in my quest to find home.

In the weeks leading up to my departure, the Taliban had taken control of Afghanistan with relative ease. Kurds watched desperate Afghans cling to a departing US aircraft, wondering if Afghanistan's fate foreshadowed their own. The presence of US combat troops in northern Iraq and northeastern Syria protected the Kurds, who are an ethnic minority in both countries. As soon as President Trump reshuffled US combat troops in northern Syria in 2019, the Turkish military and Turkish-backed Syrian Arab militias shelled civilian Kurdish areas in Syria. US combat troops were due to leave Iraq by the end of 2021. If US combat troops fully withdrew from Iraq, Kurds worried they would be targeted either by Iranian-backed militias, who believed the Kurds had helped the US assassinate Qasem Soleimani, or by ISIS, who still occasionally attacked Kirkuk and other areas. Watching the Afghan army disintegrate as soon as the US combat troops left reminded Kurds of how the Iraqi army had collapsed in 2014 in the face of ISIS.

In the meantime, the political situation in our city was precarious. Since the 2017 death of Mam Jalal Talabani, the leader of the Patriotic Union of Kurdistan (PUK), Mam Jalal's son Bafel and his nephew Lahur were fighting over power succession in the

PUK. In July of 2021, Bafel accused Lahur of corruption, insinuated Lahur was behind an assassination attempt on him, and tried to forced Lahur to leave the city. Lahur, beloved by locals because he had always lived in Kurdistan and people believed he ran the party according to PUK values whereas Bafel was raised abroad and locals thought he had sold out to the Barzanis, refused to go. Bafel organized dozens of gunmen to storm Lahur's media office and shut it down. Heads of the counterterrorism and intelligence forces loyal to Lahur were ousted and replaced by people loyal to Bafel. Lahur accused Bafel of trying to use government forces to drive him from his home in Sulaimaniyah but Bafel deflected the accusations, saying the PUK party had ordered Lahur to leave.

Lahur owned the Lalazar hotel, and his home was behind it. The university sent out an email advising us to stay away from the entire neighborhood, which was a short walk from our apartment block. New security checkpoints were set up along the road outside our compound, and there was a heavy military presence on the side streets. In late August, the PUK politburo ordered Lahur to leave the region within three days, and to stay away until two weeks after the results of the upcoming October 10 Iraqi parliamentary elections were announced. Lahur refused to budge.

I was desperate to go to the Lalazar restaurant one last time before I left on September 2. Not only was I hostage to my need to be where the action is, but Lalazar was gorged with personal nostalgia. It was the first place Luke had taken me when I arrived in 2015 and where I had taken him for a farewell dinner of margarita-fueled confession and poetry the week before he died. I had spent every Thursday evening there between 2018 and 2019 with two guy-pals, a Brit teaching at another university and a Belgian working for an Italian aid organization. My great love and I had had our first date there, two strangers searching each other for recognition between our sentences, and subsequent dates, when we shared a chance at love like a dark joke. Kayla, Kaia, and I had drunk countless latinos on Lalazar's rooftop, from which Sulaimaniyah appeared as a metropolis decked out in fairytale lights instead of a daytime city of faded glory. Sometimes, when I thought about my experiences in Sulaimaniyah, they seemed like a fabricated backstory that belonged to someone else. I wanted to go to Lalazar one last time to ground the phantom rustle of memories the way you grab onto the shards of a dream upon waking. But, because of the media coverage and warnings, none of my friends would come with me.

Overcome by a tangle of impulses, I went to Lalazar despite the political upheaval. The residential roads leading through the upscale neighborhood to the hotel were quiet. A military jeep with five or six Peshmerga, some sitting in it and others standing around it with their rifles at their sides, was parked halfway up a street which dead-ended at the hotel's entrance. Beyond the hotel, the Windex blue sky was darkening into blueberry pie filling as the sun disappeared below the horizon. The soldiers eyeballed me as I walked past, carrying my computer. I called out the standard greeting of "Choni bashi" (How are you?), which was met with uncharacteristic silence.

Another Peshmerga soldier was stationed at the hotel's entrance, but he didn't stop me as I walked into the lobby, which smelled of mildew and instinct. I greeted the receptionist and took the elevator to the top floor, where the restaurant was located. Because of the warnings, I expected the dining room to be mostly empty, but more than half the tables were full of Kurdish men. Lalazar catered to foreigners and was popular among wealthier Kurds, so it was common to see families dining, but now, there were no other women in sight. I stood at the entrance, watching the restaurant manager whisper conspiratorially to a subordinate. From where I stood, he could have been telling a dirty joke.

I caught his eye, and he came over to seat me. He explained that the rooftop wasn't open due to security concerns, and most of the men sitting in the dining room were counterterrorism and security personnel loyal to Lahur. They had been staying at the hotel during Bafel and Lahur's power struggle. In my mind, I likened the hotel to a kind of securocratic favela, which made it all the more interesting. The manager led me to a table near a window from where I could look down on Lahur's compound and see dozens of Peshmerga guarding it. If common sense had prevailed, I would have left. I sat down, ordered a latino, popped open the alibi of my computer, and kept watch on the compound and the dining room. Nothing much was happening.

Stray thoughts caught in my computer keyboard like cookie crumbs. I had sat at this table with Hasan when I interviewed him for an article I wrote after he had been my student. He once told me how he had always wanted to have a steak dinner and a glass of red wine like he had seen characters in Hollywood films do. As a thank you for letting me interview him, I treated him to a platonic Lalazar steak one Saturday afternoon. On another afternoon, a quartet of students took me to Lalazar's rooftop after their finals to say thank you. Over chicken Caesar salad made without any lettuce (courtesy of another cholera outbreak), they remarked how they longed for the days of Saddam because "at least he kept the country functioning."

My heart broadened as my mind spun a carousel of student faces. The 10SP kids from the international school in Erbil, in those pre-ISIS days when Kurdistan seemed gleaming and implausible. How those kids swerved me from homicidal to enchanted and back again, over and over, much like love. The undergraduate course I taught when I first arrived at the university and how the students and I gave ourselves over to the intimacy of risk to fully mine Margaret Atwood's and Carol Ann Duffy's worlds. The adult learners in the professional development institute, especially Othman, who called me on Facebook messenger one night from Basra. Terrified, he was crouched low in the back seat of his uncle's car while an Iranian-backed militia shot up the street, and one again in his young life, he hoped not to die. My first cohort in the academic preparatory program, whom I proudly saw receive their university diplomas four years later. The resilience of the 2017 cohort, who continued a demanding academic schedule amidst violent conflict, heartbreak, and political chaos. My spring 2018 cohort, chock full of bright, ambitious female students who, for the first time in my teaching experience in Kurdistan, outnumbered the male students. They symbolized a hopeful future for a more gender-equitable Iraq. My Yazidi students whose lives had been upended by ISIS. My Syrian-Kurdish students whose lives had been upended by the Turkish military or Turkish-back Syrian Arab militias. My Iraqi students whose lives had been upended first by the US-led coalition forces and later by ISIS. Watching them persevere without self-pity or rancor and carry joy and gratitude despite enduring hardship helped me grow up. My fall 2019 cohort, with whom I spent five hours a day, five days a week for 12 weeks. They were the last group I taught before the pandemic made a mockery of academic standards in favor of retention rates to keep tuition dollars flowing. The 2020 and 2021 students who didn't quit school during the pandemic despite online learning being frustrating and lonely. These were the faces that knew me and helped me know myself. As memories orbited, I thought again about novelist Fred Buechner's theory: we find our true vocation where our deep gladness meets the world's great need. I realized I had been living a real life in northern Iraq, and now I was leaving it. I felt like a secondhand book: tattered and *itinerant*.

Living and working in northern Iraq had been a big part of my identity for the better part of a decade. It emblemized the choices I had made pursuing something elusive, and it was a people magnet. My East German partner fell for the intrigue as he half-jokingly accused me of being some kind of American spy when we first met. At a long table of interdisciplinary artists at an art residency outside of Barcelona, I fielded questions ranging from how I dated to if I was scared to what I wore. My Chicago-based dentist wondered where I had gotten my suntan and laughed uproariously when I explained laying out in a kiddie pool while fighting off pigeons on our balcony. When I was on a Chicago radio show in 2019 to promote my novel *Moxie*, the interviewer and I talked mostly about Iraq, which had nothing to do with the book, as did other interviewers. Living in Iraq made me *interesting*. As a remote worker with a time-scratched face starting over in a new professional field in a new place at the age of 54, who was I? What I had to offer was what I had lived.

As I kept watch on the compound, an old urban dance song played in Lalazar's dining room, pulling me back in time to a party in a private house with a bigger collection of Kurdish books than the city's library. I am with my friend who owns a popular Lebanese restaurant in town. We arrive late, having come from dinner with a Canadian oil executive hosting two mercenaries, an evangelical Texan and a Glaswegian obsessed with talking about his butthole, both of whom had overstayed their visas fighting ISIS. My friend's ex and her friends theatrically stare at us as we enter the house party. We surf over their unlaundered piles of envy, curling into dislike, and glide onto the dance floor. Dancing feels like flying. In the bubble of breath and body we form, there is exhilaration and release. I have never felt so alive, so complete, so free.

Cheat Sheet

Asayish: Kurdistan's intelligence and special security police.

EFL: English as a Foreign Language. It differs from **ESL** (English as a Second Language) because a country where EFL is taught is not an English-speaking country.

Erbil: The capital of the Kurdistan Region of Iraq (KRI) and the de facto stronghold of the ruling Barzani family and the Kurdistan Democratic Party (KDP, also known as the PDK).

Haram: Forbidden by Islamic law.

Hectare: a metric unit of area equal to a square with 100-meter sides. There are one hundred hectares in one square kilometer. Hectares are used to measure land.

IDP: Internally displaced persons. A term for people who flee war and violence within their own country. Unlike refugees, IDPs do not cross a national border.

KDP: The Kurdistan Democratic Party, also known as the PDK. One of two major political parties in Kurdistan. The KDP is led by the Barzani family and based in Erbil, Kurdistan.

KRG: The Kurdistan Regional Government. The KRG is the official government of the autonomous Kurdish Region of northern Iraq (KRI).

KRI: The Kurdistan Region of Iraq, an autonomous region within Iraq. The area outside the KRI is often referred to as **the south**, meaning the area south of Kurdistan and under control of Iraq's central government in Baghdad.

latino: (small l): a drink made with a lager beer, tequila, and lemon juice.

NGO: a non-governmental organization. NGOs are typically non-profit organizations, working in the humanitarian aid sector.

Peshmerga: The Kurdish military forces of the autonomous Kurdish Region of Iraq. Peshmerga do not report to a central command. Rather, they are under the command of the political parties to which they are allied.

PKK: The Kurdistan Workers' Party. The PKK is a Kurdish militant political organization and armed guerilla movement fighting for Kurdish rights within Turkey.

PMF: Popular Mobilization Forces, also known as Popular Mobilization Units (**PMU**). The PMF are predominantly made up of Shia Muslims and were instrumental in defeating ISIS in Iraq.

PUK: Patriotic Union of Kurdistan. The other major political party in Kurdistan. The PUK was founded by Mam Jalal Talabani, Fuad Masum, Nawshirwan Mustafa, Ali Askari, and Adel Murad. It is the major political party in Sulaimaniyah, Kurdistan.

Sulaimaniyah (also spelled Sulaimania, Slemani and Sulaimani): Kurdistan's second most important city after Erbil, located near the Iraq-Iran border. It is the de facto stronghold of the Talabani family and the Patriotic Union of Kurdistan (PUK).

TOEFL: Test of English as a Foreign Language. A standardized test to measure English language ability in non-native speakers.

Wasta: Nepotism fueled by the power of connections, often based on a family's last name.

Yazidi: An ethnoreligious minority whose ancestral homeland is near Mount Sinjar in northern Iraq. In 2014, ISIS attacked the Yazidis, killing Yazidi men and enslaving women and children in a genocidal campaign.

YPG: The People's Protection Units. A Kurdish militia which leads the Syrian Democratic Forces (SDF), an alliance of forces formed during the Syrian Civil War. The YPG were instrumental in defeating ISIS in Syria.

Acknowledgements

I would have never written *Breakfast Wine* if I had not been an artist in residence at the Atlantic Center for the Arts. Telling stories over dinner one night, master artist Randall Silvis and the other writers in residence, Mary Jane Pories, Kevin OttemFox, Neal Coomer, Ge Gao, and Christopher Linforth, encouraged me to start writing about my time in Iraq. For the next workshop submission, I brought in the essay "Reprieve" which later became "Don't Say a Word", "Down the Rabbit Hole", and "The Impossible Do-Over" as I refined the structure of *Breakfast Wine*. Without their push, I would not have embarked on writing this book. I also want to thank master artist Charlie Hailey, who was working with a different group of interdisciplinary artists at the residency. I drew on his work and our conversations for "Camping."

Breakfast Wine would also not exist without journalist Karen Emslie's invaluable feedback and constant cheerleading. Thank you, Karen for never tiring of my question, "Is this boring?" Thank you also for asking the kinds of questions that made me probe deeper, interrogate, and flesh out ideas hiding in plain sight.

I am indebted to the kindness of the people I have known in Kurdistan, Iraq, especially to my students: Lara, Nara, Zerin, Sardilla, Sanna, Mariam, Sara I., Sarah, Dilvin, Marley, Shamil, Rohz, Ayob, Bader, Sara, Yousif, Hamza, Hasan, Omar, Omar A., Hallo, Shorshvan, Azade, Kanee, Osaed, Mohammad, Mohammed, Muhammad, Abdulbasit, Mina, Las, Hawar, Naji, Sima, Kardo, Sarmad, Meer, Binaee, Bakr, Lilyan, Balen, Mardin,

Sawen, Shams, Yousif T, Sirood, and many others. You all brought me so much joy in the classroom. I appreciate how open you were when you shared about your culture and your lives. I value your trust. I really miss your hugs.

I also want to thank my colleagues and other adventurers, many of whom I am lucky to call lifelong friends. Katy, Michael Paul, Maria, Roy, Shaun, Daria, Saad, Martina, Nancy, Hayley, Rachel R, Holly, Chris, Cris, Nino, Tim, Tim R., Toon, Ian, Jessica, and of course, Pete: We went through some shit together. Thanks for pulling me through.

Reading is essential to my writing process. Taking another writer's words and rhythms into myself unblocks me so I can write from my emotional truth to investigate my material. In a way, the act of writing continues a conversation. Working on *Breakfast Wine*, I was in conversation with Mikel Jollett, John Long, Colum McCann, Don Chaon, David Brooks, John Washington, Anna Badkhen, Kenneth Cain, Heidi Postelwait, Andrew Thomson, Kim Barker, Jeffrey Gettleman, Margaret Attwood, and others. A big thanks to Karen Kilgariff and Georgia Hardstark, who coined the term "breakfast wine" on their podcast *My Favorite Murder*.

A huge thanks to writer and journalist Jere Van Dyk for being an amazing mentor and pushing me to go to Iraq, one of the best decisions I have ever made.

You can write a book, but if it isn't published, no one reads it. Thanks to Apprentice House Press, under the careful stewardship of Kevin Atticks, for giving *Breakfast Wine* a home. Thanks to Molly Gerard for her kind edits, Jack Stromberg for internal design, Louis Mandrapilias for the book cover, and to publicist Sheryl Johnston for helping *Breakfast Wine* be known.

Thanks to my mother, Donna K. Poppe, and my late father, Fred W. Poppe, with whom all my writing began.

About the Author

Alex Poppe is the author of four works of literary fiction: *Duende* by Regal House Publishing, *Jinwar and Other Stories* by Cune Press, *Moxie* by Tortoise Books, and *Girl, World* by Laughing Fire Press. *Duende* won the 2024 American Legacy Book Awards in the novella category, the 2023 International Book Awards in the novella category, and was a 2023 Spring Readers' Choice Book Awards finalist. *Jinwar and Other Stories* was a runner up for the 2024 PenCraft Book Awards, won the 2023 Spring Readers' Choice Book Award in the adult book category and was a 2022 International Book Awards finalist. In 2018, *Girl, World* was named a 35 Over 35 Debut Book Award winner, First Horizon Award finalist, Montaigne Medal finalist, Eric Hoffer Grand Prize finalist, and was awarded an Honorable Mention in General Fiction from the Eric Hoffer Awards. Her short fiction and non-fiction have been nominated for the Pushcart Prize, Best of the Net, and commended for the Baker Prize among others. In 2021, Alex was an artist-in-residence at the Atlantic Center for the Arts, where *Breakfast Wine* began.

Apprentice House Press
Loyola University Maryland

Apprentice House is the country's only campus-based, student-staffed book publishing company. Directed by professors and industry professionals, it is a nonprofit activity of the Communication Department at Loyola University Maryland.

Using state-of-the-art technology and an experiential learning model of education, Apprentice House publishes books in untraditional ways. This dual responsibility as publishers and educators creates an unprecedented collaborative environment among faculty and students, while teaching tomorrow's editors, designers, and marketers.

Eclectic and provocative, Apprentice House titles intend to entertain as well as spark dialogue on a variety of topics. Financial contributions to sustain the press's work are welcomed. Contributions are tax deductible to the fullest extent allowed by the IRS.

To learn more about Apprentice House books or to obtain submission guidelines, please visit www.apprenticehouse.com.

Apprentice House Press
Communication Department
Loyola University Maryland
4501 N. Charles Street
Baltimore, MD 21210
Ph: 410-617-5265
info@apprenticehouse.com • www.apprenticehouse.com

www.ingramcontent.com/pod-product-compliance
Lightning Source LLC
Chambersburg PA
CBHW050106170426
43198CB00014B/2477